CREATIVE, INC.

CREATIVE, INC.

The Ultimate Guide to Running
a Successful Freelance Business

MEG MATEO ILASCO &
JOY DEANGDEELERT CHO

CHRONICLE BOOKS
SAN FRANCISCO

Library of Congress Cataloging-in-Publication Data:
Ilasco, Meg Mateo.
    Creative, inc. : the ultimate guide to running a successful freelance
  business / Meg Mateo Ilasco and Joy Deangdeelert Cho. – 1st ed.
        p. cm.
    ISBN 978-0-8118-7161-7
    1. Art–Vocational guidance. I. Cho, Joy Deangdeelert. II. Title.

  N8350.I42 2010
  707–dc22

                                    2009032756

Manufactured in Singapore
Designed by Oh Joy! Studio

10 9 8 7 6 5 4 3 2 1

Chronicle Books LLC
680 Second Street
San Francisco, California 94107
www.chroniclebooks.com

To our husbands—Marvin and Bob,

Thank you for not only being our partners in life but also for being
our biggest fans. Thanks for your love, support, patience, and humor
with our nontraditional career choices.

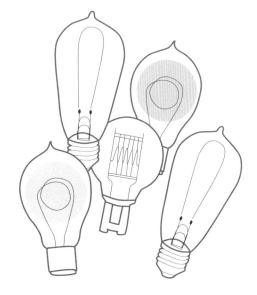

Contents

Introduction

Freelancing is a leap of faith. Announce to your friends and family that you're quitting your day job to freelance and it's unlikely that congratulations will come from every angle. For the more traditional types (read: Mom and Dad), the idea of turning down a steady paycheck to pursue a career doing what many would consider just a creative hobby sounds like a risky venture. To others, the word *freelance* conjures romantic images of Carrie Bradshaw types waiting for assignments as they sip decaf caramel machiatos at the corner cafe. While there may be truth to both viewpoints, the reality of creative freelancing is that it gives you the unique opportunity to put your individual talents to work and earn a living while you're at it. Enjoying what you do for a living doesn't have to be an idle dream.

As the new kid to freelancing, you will learn the rules of the playground and the pitfalls to avoid. Whether you're a designer, illustrator, animator, stylist, photographer, or other creative, we'll show you how to set up your business, promote your work, find and work with clients, set your fees, acquire an agent, and handle your bookkeeping. We'll also get into the nitty-gritty of partnering, balancing your personal and work life, and what to do when things are going so well that you have to expand your business. From the interviews of the experienced self-employed creatives in this book, you'll learn about freelancing directly from the source, discovering that the journey to being a successful freelancer begins differently for everyone. Some have degrees from art school, while others cultivated their education on their own. Some start by accident, others out of sheer drive, while still others find freelancing as the silver lining in an otherwise adverse situation, such as a layoff. Through it all, though, you'll learn lessons through their hiccups and victories.

Freelancing is by no means a quick and easy pursuit. More than likely, you'll be going at it alone, which means making decisions on your own. But there are certainly advantages to being autonomous. You can change the characteristics of your business at a moment's notice and turn down unappealing assignments when they just don't fit. But be clear with yourself about the reasons you're getting into freelancing. If you're leaving your day job because it's too much work or too stressful, be aware that freelancing may require even more hours and carry even greater pressure.

Switching from a steady job to a work life filled with new clientele and unexpected (often daily) changes can be daunting. Fortunately for you, we'll prepare you for this new lifestyle and warn you about potential stumbling blocks and how to overcome them.

All this raises the question "Why put myself through the stress of starting and running my own business?" The answer is a matter of payoff. Making your passion pay is a gamble—but the greater the stakes, the greater the rewards, both financially and creatively. Though you'll probably be working more hours than ever, you'll work with artistic freedom on a larger variety of projects than you'd probably have if you were on staff somewhere, and you'll have the potential to earn more money with every commission. You'll soon see why people who become freelancers would use the word *liberating* to describe a career move that does not immediately produce a bigger paycheck. Surely, as your client base grows, more money will come. But for passionate freelancers, money isn't the only goal. It's the happiness derived from a sense of purpose and the excitement that comes with the challenges of every new project. Freelancing takes vision, dedication, hard work, organization, business savvy, and, of course, a true love of your art. In this book, we'll give you the guidance you need to turn your creative skills into a full-fledged freelance career. In time, you'll become a part of a rare group of people whose career represents a creative extension of themselves, who never have a case of the Mondays, and who haven't looked back since taking the freelance leap.

INTRODUCTION
TO CREATIVE FREELANCING

CHAPTER

1

Do you ever wonder where your talents would take you if you put just as much effort (if not more) into working for yourself as you do working for someone else? If testing your creative potential has crossed your mind, it's likely that freelancing could be that change you've been searching for. Freelancing offers you the opportunity to shape your career however you like. You can choose your clients, how much you want to work, what type of work to do, and how much to charge. Freelancing means you'll no longer be clocking in hours for the Man; you'll be turning your art into a full-time career and working for the best boss of all, You. In this chapter you'll find out the qualities you need to succeed and determine whether the creative freelancing lifestyle is for you.

What Is Creative Freelancing?

We define *creative freelancer* as someone who is a self-employed subcontractor offering her creative services to buyers. Typically a solitary practice, creative freelancing can be a group effort as well: whether a group of colleagues or a husband-and-wife team, freelancers can band together as a collective or form a partnership. However you do it, creative freelancing requires you to step up to the dual challenge of producing effective visual communications and managing a business. Remember, just because you are embarking on an artistic career without suits and ties, or even walls, that doesn't mean you should use your newly found freedom to operate your venture on the fly. To succeed, you have to manage your freelance business with the same level of seriousness as that of a corporate CEO. You simply can't rely on your talents alone. You need to know as much about managing a business as you do about your art. Luckily, you'll find everything you need to get started here.

NINE QUALITIES OF A SUCCESSFUL FREELANCER

How do you know if you're freelance material? It's a vocation that's not for everyone. You need to be self-motivated, self-reliant, organized, confident, and an effective communicator. You may not possess all these characteristics right now, but with practice and a little discipline you can certainly develop them and be on your way to freelance success.

01 Strong business sense

Creative freelancing is not just about producing good work. It's essential to develop a strong business acumen as well. There's enough ego and talent coursing through the creative world for even the most gifted artist to get lost in the crowd. The ones who flex their business muscle become the most identifiable and successful. Even though you'll have more freedom than the typical nine-to-fiver, freelancing carries all the responsibilities of an independent business, including marketing, accounting, and office management. When you're running a business, you'll find yourself having to make many solo decisions at any given point, so you'll have to be a confident decision maker. You will also need self-motivation and resourcefulness to maintain your own schedule and provide structure to your workday—qualities that will come in handy when you're chasing down payments from clients!

02 A love of your art

Maybe your career has been moving along briskly at a motion-graphics firm, but the road ahead holds little appeal and autonomy is the only move that makes sense. Maybe you took illustration gigs during college, and with graduation around the corner you're ready to make a full-time go of it. Or maybe you were laid off, and this misfortune has presented an opportunity to make an exciting change. However you came to the decision to freelance, one thing is certain: you have to be passionate about what you do. Ask yourself these questions: Would freelancing excite you enough to get you out of bed in the morning? Would you mind sometimes burning the midnight oil to finish a project? Could you be happy turning your creative outlet into your main source of income? If you're drawn to freelancing mainly because of the lifestyle, the lure of authorship, or the potential for fame, you'll likely become frustrated and burn out quickly when success doesn't happen overnight. A successful freelancer is passionate about his art and seeks inspiration to fuel it—even in his off-duty hours—simply for the sake of generating work that he loves.

03 Curiosity

Because you're a visual auteur and an idea person, your curiosity has probably gotten you to where you are right now. Curiosity keeps your mind primed as a creative tool, keeps you open to new ways of working and looking at things. Truth be told, though, the more you become an expert in your field, the less time you'll have to step outside it and engage with the rest of the world. This disconnect can affect how you deal with people or approach problems. That's why you need to continue to make an effort to stay curious and connected: read newspapers and books, watch documentaries and movies, and attend cultural events, to name a few. Whether you're a film director or graphic designer, at some point you'll probably be assigned a project dealing with subject matter you're not familiar with. If you're an illustrator hoping to land your artwork in the *New York Times* or any other news outlet, you should be fully aware of current events so that you can tackle a news-related illustration with ease. The more diverse your experiences and interests, the stronger your ability to come up with ideas and translate your client's needs into a successful piece of work.

04 Confidence and a strong vision

A strong freelancer does much more than simply execute the instructions of an editor or art director. If you let the client dictate the entire project through a paint-by-numbers program, you'll feel like a trained art monkey. You must have the confidence to suggest your own ideas and bring your voice into the conversation. This type of creative bravura doesn't mean that an in-your-face personal style should dominate every project. Success will most likely come with a fine balance between articulating your vision and taking into account your client's needs. To earn a living, you won't always get to pick and choose commissions that allow you to express 100 percent of your creative vision. And that's okay. When you need an outlet for that self-possessed creative energy, take it upon yourself to initiate personal projects that reflect your particular style. As you add more of these personal designs to your portfolio, you'll start attracting clients eager for your specific point of view.

05 Good listening and observational skills

In the service world, the customer is king. Though you may have a strong vision, operating on the credo "Do whatever you want, when you want" will do nothing to serve your client. Remember that, to stay in business, you'll need to please your client before pleasing yourself. But, as we outlined in the preceding section, you'll need to be receptive to your client's needs without letting the client run all over you. With keen observational and listening skills, you'll find a vision that satisfies both you and your client. The more you understand the client's point of view and what they're hoping to achieve, the wider the net you can cast to solve the problem. In fact, creative epiphanies are more likely to happen when there is complete understanding. Plus, clients will respect you more when they feel you clearly understand their needs, and that is key to developing a strong relationship. Despite the surplus of talent available, buyers like working with freelancers they know and trust. If you are talented, and you're a good listener and an agreeable person, it's likely you will be commissioned for future jobs.

06 Good communication skills

When it comes to working with clients, you cannot rely on visuals as your sole mode of communication. In the ideation phase, before proper visuals are available, it's essential for you to inspire and persuade your client with words, whether written or in conversation. The same goes for working with clients who may not be visually literate in your field. Oftentimes, clients don't know exactly what they are buying or what they want until it's delivered. So you'll need to be able to articulate your artistic vision and direction. Throughout the process, it is critical to understand and explain why you took a certain approach. If a customer questions your approach, you should be able to say, "I feel that this is the right direction, and here's why."

07 An ability to handle criticism and rejection

It happens to all of us. Even the most established creative freelancers have produced work that doesn't quite meet their client's expectations. Your work won't always be a slam-dunk, so be ready to digest less-than-enthusiastic reviews sometimes. In an intensely competitive arena, all freelancers are bound to encounter rejection—from agents, clients, and even peers they may turn to for feedback. Hearing criticism isn't always easy. You'll need to thicken your skin and remember that it's business—not a personal attack. Your client needs to put his or her business agenda first. It may take some time, but a successful freelancer eventually learns to take criticism and turn it into a result that pleases the client. Getting to that point in your career may require some sweat and tears, but it will make each victory all the more meaningful.

08 A positive attitude and professional demeanor

A good attitude is priceless when you are running your own business. It's important to handle every job, whether small or large, with joie de vivre. Whether you're interacting with clients or vendors or simply reflecting on a challenge, a negative attitude won't make anything any better. Clients don't respond well to people who get easily upset or let unexpected situations ruin their day. And remember, mistakes are part of the discovery process. So do your best to stay positive, no matter what unexpected problems arise.

0⑨ Good work habits

Good work habits lead to better work, and better work leads to more projects and more clients. If organization has never been your strong point, it's time for a change. If you work from home, turn off the TV and keep personal interests like surfing the Internet, listening to the news, or reading magazines to a minimum. Stay focused on business by making a list of tasks to accomplish every day. And clients appreciate quality work that is done quickly, so challenge your efficiency: try to beat the deadline by completing a job in five days instead of eight. As a freelancer, you have to be self-motivated, because only you can set the bar for your skill and output.

NO DEGREE? NO WORRIES!

If you're worried because you don't have an art degree, fret not. There's no doubt you'll need a sharp creative eye and training in mechanical skills—whether that means learning your way around a 3-D modeling program, mastering a digital SLR camera, or tackling Adobe Premiere Pro—to become a creative freelancer. But how you acquire those skills is not as important as your talent and execution. So whether your education comes from a well-known art school or online camera tutorials, it should have no bearing on your success as a freelancer. Many successful freelancers, including a few profiled in this book, are self-taught. Your artistic portfolio is the equalizer, and it counts for far more than pedigree does. Certainly there are benefits to enrolling in a structured academic program, such as a well-rounded education, not to mention contacts and recommendations from your fellow students and professors. However, with an accurate assessment of your strengths and weaknesses, you can educate yourself in your field, taking classes or reading books in the areas where you need to improve. You can also duplicate the camaraderie found at school by immersing yourself in online communities of like-minded creatives through blogs, forums, and social networking sites.

Preparing for Freelancing

Once you make the decision to freelance, it's likely you'll want to start immediately. But before you march into your boss's office with a resignation letter, it's essential that you gather as much information as possible to set yourself up for success. Preparation is everything. There are plenty of things you can do to lay the groundwork while you're still holding down your day job or finishing up with school.

• Actively research and get to know your industry. Scan through books, trade publications, and Web sites to find companies you'd be interested in working with and whose style matches your own. If you're not sure whether they hire freelancers, you may have to contact them directly. Pay close attention to the types of talent businesses seek out and take note of the companies you think would be most interested in your work.

• Find out which events, such as conferences, your ideal clients or practitioners attend. Go to these events to make connections. Collect information to establish a network of colleagues and set up a database of potential clients.

• Read up on the lives and work of other creative freelancers in your field. Start here with the freelancers profiled in this book. Did they go to school, or are they self-taught? Which clients are they working with? What was critical to their success? As you discover the answers to these questions, that will help inspire and prepare you for the path ahead.

As you begin this endeavor, embrace your newness to the freelance game. Don't get discouraged by how green you are, and don't let the achievements of others deflate you. As you flip through design annuals, scan through photography blogs, or check out online reels, you may envy established freelancers working with big-name clients or ogle work and wonder, "Why didn't I think of that?" Remember that at one time all these creatives were in your shoes. Take their success stories as inspiration. As a new freelancer, you'll probably have to pay your dues—possibly by compromising your vision or accepting uninspiring projects just to pay the bills. The road to a profitable freelance career doing cutting-edge work may not always be the swiftest, but if you keep building your body of work with an emphasis on quality, prized clients with meaningful commissions will soon be knocking on your door.

Andrew Bannecker's story has all the makings of a freelancer's fairy tale. In 2001, soon after graduating from Wichita State University with a degree in communications, he realized that his calling was in art and design. In true underdog style, he created his own artistic education, building a body of artwork that was purely self-taught and self-initiated. Eight years, six cities, and umpteen art and non-art jobs later, Andrew is now a full-time freelance illustrator represented by agencies in Europe and the United States, with commissions from clients such as Starbucks, HarperCollins, and Target under his belt. Not bad for a Kansas native who dabbled in graphic design and started undergrad with the belief that he was going to be a zookeeper. Andrew's story is a lesson in the benefits of a go-getter mentality, proving that your trajectory can only head skyward when hard work, momentum, and serendipity are on your side.

Before you were an illustrator, you were a graphic designer. How did you get design jobs without a degree in graphic design?
I enrolled in one graphic design class in college, which on the first day required me to draw circles. I was young and ignorant and found the exercise boring, so I dropped out of the class. I decided that graphic design wasn't for me, and I ended up with a degree in communications. A few years after graduation, I moved back to Wichita with a renewed interest in graphic design. I didn't have any training, so I started teaching myself how to do logos and layouts—and did it all in Photoshop. I fell in love with graphic design. I started a Web site with a portfolio of these self-initiated projects I had been playing around with. It caught the attention of a local design and branding agency called the Greteman Group. I was very surprised and excited when they offered me my first salaried design job.

How did you get into illustration?

I had a fantastic job in Washington, D.C., working for Arnold Worldwide, a multimillion dollar advertising agency. It was a job I got completely by accident when a friend offered to drop off my portfolio and they later hired me as a designer. On a project we were doing for Amacai, they needed a poster made, so I illustrated it. This was my first attempt at illustration. The poster won several awards, and it opened my mind to pursuing illustration as a career.

How did you go from illustrating on your own to being represented by an agency?

While working as an art director at a marketing firm in Chicago, I began working on my illustration portfolio on the side. Every night after work, I spent time exploring and creating illustrations. Having worked for several advertising agencies helped me understand how to make illustrations that were commercial and marketable. Once I felt I had a decent portfolio, I researched illustration agencies and came across the Central Illustration Agency [CIA], based in London. I felt like my work was a good fit with the other illustrators they represented. They were my top choice, but I also contacted other agencies as well. I basically e-mailed everyone with a link to my Web site. Some agencies rejected me, but CIA loved my work and saw the fit. I was giddy at the notion that an agency in London would sign me on. The first commission I got from CIA was from Starbucks.

How did you juggle your day job and your burgeoning illustration career?

It was definitely a balancing act. I juggled the new illustration career with CIA and the responsibilities of working as an art director for almost two years. I had to be strategic—scheduling phone meetings in the mornings before work (the London-Chicago time difference was challenging) and working on projects until 3 A.M. Though I felt like I was managing a million deadlines, I was able to stay on top of things. I developed a reputation for sending work fast. If clients needed something in three days, I would turn it around in one day. I made sure that I was someone who was easy to work with. Soon the illustration commissions started trickling in, and when suddenly more and more came my way, I realized that I could do this full-time.

You lived in New York for a while. Was that move strategic?

Yes. As my illustration career was growing, it seemed like a logical next step—especially after Bernstein & Andriulli [BA], the U.S. sister agency of CIA, signed me on. They are based in New York, so I thought being close to them would be a great opportunity to build a relationship. I got to know my agents personally. And it's great because when something came up, I was immediately available. BA hosts parties where they sometimes have a meet-and-greet with artists, and I had the chance to meet current or potential clients. If I lived elsewhere at the time, I probably wouldn't have had the chance to go to these events.

What kinds of promotional activity do you do?

The good thing about having an agent is that they manage most of the promotional activity. They create a marketing plan for the year and figure out what your involvement will be—whether it's creating an illustration for a tote bag or choosing artwork for a direct mail piece. They're incredibly helpful and have a ton of clients on their mailing list. Other than that, my Web site and blog, which I upload with new work constantly, is what I do to promote myself.

As a self-taught illustrator, what suggestions do you have for someone who wants to acquire skills in illustration? Do you feel there are benefits to going to art school?

I don't necessarily think you would be a better artist if you went to art school—I don't feel [not having gone] has been a handicap for me. In fact, most people think that I did go to art school. One benefit of going to school is that you get a lot of contacts. You get to know fellow artists as well as having the benefit of teachers who are already in the field. My advice to aspiring illustrators who didn't go or can't afford to go to art school is to develop your own unique style. It has to be recognizable and current. You have to continue to grow as an artist, and your style must keep evolving. You also have to remember that you are a commercial artist and not a fine artist, so your work has to be marketable. Most important, you should never stop creating your own work—put in the hours on self-initiated projects. At least in my experience, personal work with no client constraints is usually going to be my best. •

Freelance Earnings

You're probably wondering how you'll make ends meet while you're starting out. It's normal to worry that you won't make enough money to pay your bills or that no one will hire you. Freelancing can be unpredictable—you might not know when you'll receive a new assignment, and, when you do get one, you can't be sure you'll be paid on time. But life without a steady paycheck doesn't have to be a nerve-racking ordeal. Stack the cards in your favor with self-promotion practices that will attract new clients, and set a budget to handle the ebbs and flows of your income. Plus, with faith in your abilities, a little elbow grease, and lots of preparation, you will find the challenges less difficult. You'll need to price your services competitively, accept some mundane commissions, and maybe even take on pro bono work, especially if you are in the portfolio-building stage. But, once demand for your work grows, you can steadily increase your prices and even turn down projects that you're not interested in.

Moonlighting

You may want to get a head start on your freelance career while you still have a full-time job, but think carefully about moonlighting. It might seem like a wise plan to freelance on the side and wait until you've built a good customer base before going full time, especially with the uncertainty freelancing brings. But juggling freelancing while holding down a steady job isn't always easy. You'll have to dedicate much of your free time to working on your freelance gigs. Moreover, clients and agents may need to schedule phone meetings during the day, while you're still committed to your day job. If a project is on a tight deadline, clients may need drafts, sketches, or prototyping within hours, and you often have to be readily available to receive feedback or answer questions via e-mail or phone. "Can you make this line thicker?" "Can we change the blue to PMS 631?" A barrage of questions and requests can come at any given moment, so it's important to make sure you have the capacity and the time to manage these demands while handling your day job.

If you don't manage this delicate balancing act well and you start to miss deadlines, you'll risk burning bridges and losing future clients. For a fledgling freelancer, it could adversely affect your potential success. That being said, if you do decide to take side gigs, here is some advice:

01 Be wary of accepting jobs with short deadlines.

02 Keep your stress level low and try to work out potential kinks in advance—schedule phone meetings before your workday begins or during your lunch hour, and know what resources (such as printers and computer workstations) are available near your place of work.

03 Most important, keep a cell phone handy at all times, especially one that can receive and send e-mail.

Freelancing Fresh Out of School

Life on the other side of the diploma doesn't necessarily greet you with a freelance career. Freelancing right out of school can be difficult without the experience that comes from having had a couple of jobs. But, for illustrators and film school grads, going straight to freelancing is pretty common.

For example, in the film industry, most jobs are filled on a contractual basis, with work ending when the project is complete. So you need only look on a job listings board to get your first taste of freelancing. Though it will likely not be the directorial debut you were hoping for, it's certainly experience that you can build on. Recent illustration grads often find themselves looking for freelance work immediately, because staff illustration jobs are less common than other types of creative positions. As a new grad, stay open to a range of projects. Every job (no matter how small) is a stepping stone to bigger and better things.

If you're still in school and are planning to take the leap into freelancing, try to land internships, part-time jobs, or commissions to get a leg up on the competition. Each of those experiences represents a contact for you when you graduate and could potentially generate more work in the future. While you're still a student, use as many of the school's facilities and free services you can to print your portfolio and marketing materials and build your Web site. Get as much feedback as you can on your portfolio from your peers and mentors. Ask your teachers (especially the ones who still actively practice their art) for recommendations for production houses or names of editors or art directors who may be interested in seeing your portfolio. Whomever you choose to ask for a recommendation must be able to stand behind your creative talent and abilities. Pick an instructor you know well and who has confidence in your work; otherwise she may be less willing to give you a recommendation.

A benefit of starting your freelance career straight from school is that you get a jump start on developing your personal aesthetic, and you won't be limited by churning out work under another company's signature style. But the best part about starting a freelance career straight from school is that you probably won't have financial security to surrender. Once you acquire more debts and bills (especially a mortgage) and get a biweekly paycheck to support them, it can be hard to give up your day job. The whiplash over the financial shift is certainly felt much more strongly by those who've gotten used to receiving regular paychecks.

"If having power means you can't work with your friends, then you really haven't got any." Those are words Frank Sinatra once uttered, and clearly, for Chris Riehl, the power of his freelance career is built on the friends he's made. Barely in his twenties, Chris began freelancing while attending Art Center College of Design in Pasadena, California. Like that of most students, his goal was just to earn enough money to pay the rent. But when classmate Brendan Wiuff proposed a collaborative project in school, Chris soon learned there was strength in numbers. Realizing they could do bigger projects together than they could do alone, Chris and Brendan, along with four other schoolmates, formed a company called Born Collective in 2005—and started raking in freelance gigs while juggling their academic life. The group is still in business, and they take their art seriously, producing projects that integrate the talents of all six individuals, proving that the end product is greater than the sum of its parts. As they've grown, they've found themselves hearkening back to the days of yore when they worked out of a crammed attic in a house they once shared. Chris's story is a clear example of how connections matter in the freelance world, and how school can be the perfect breeding ground for developing them.

When did you start freelancing, and who was your first client?

I got my first freelancing job while I was at school. A close and longtime friend of mine introduced me to his friends looking for a freelancer at their design studio called Nanospore. I needed the money, and, like most students, I was willing to do work on the cheap. I ended up helping to create a viral ad for Nike, their client. Other jobs came from that, as friends of friends started to refer me. They'd say, "I saw the work you did for Nike—can you do something similar for me?"

How did the Born Collective come together?

Born Collective started in 2005, while I was at Art Center. I met Brendan Wiuff, a talented illustrator, who created these character-driven graphic novels called *The Braver*. I had been taking a reel animation class, and he asked me if I could take on his graphic novel as the subject for my class. At first I was skeptical, but he sold me on the idea, and I made this short title sequence to a fake cartoon. During the process, I fell in love with his artwork and the process of working together. We then decided to start our own company and got four other guys, Matthew Encina, Jiaren Hui, Aaron Bjork, and Michael Relth, to join the collective. Together we were able to pull in jobs to pay the rent. Many times we were underpaid, but all these jobs and connections paid in dividends later in our careers. The good thing about working collectively is that you're able to do bigger and more complicated projects that would be impossible to do alone.

How difficult was it to juggle your schoolwork with freelance jobs?

It got crazy in school. Matt, Mike, and I lived in a house together, and our attic became the Born headquarters. There were times when one of us would have to fly to Scottsdale to deliver a project when homework was due the next day. Or we'd be at a client meeting and then have to rush back to school in time for a critique. Our teachers were well aware of what we were doing, and we did get some stern words at times. We were also able to extend our group method of working into our schoolwork. We would write up proposals to tell our instructors what we would be making as a group to satisfy their class requirements. For the most part, they were very supportive of our group mentality.

At Art Center, the focus tends to be on the individual. But what you find out when you go out into the real world, especially in the animation industry, is that no one does anything by themselves—authorship is shared by a lot of people. We just got a head start on that experience.

How does Born work? Does everyone have a particular role in Born?

It's a very socialist setup, and we are all equal partners. People are allowed to work both with the collective and individually. For projects we do collectively, we switch around roles and wear different hats. For some projects, I may get the creative director spot, while for others, I might get the animator spot, and so on. It changes. We may have a different role every time, but regardless we all have to work.

How beneficial was going to art school for your career?

Of course, Art Center was crucial for getting Born Collective together. But our professors were also key to our success, especially for the connections and resources they offered. For example, we got this gig doing motion graphics for Linkin Park. For their 2008 world tour, they asked us to create graphics for the JumboTron that would sync with their song "In Pieces." It wasn't until much later that we found out our department chair, Nikolaus Hafermaas, had referred us for the gig. Nik also set me up with *Step* magazine, which resulted in Born's selection in their 2008 emerging talents issue. Also, some of the faculty at Art Center run some of the nicer studios around town. So if I don't know something—for instance, if the budget a client is offering us is appropriate—I can call on some of my old professors or people I used to go to school with. We are not a part of any guild or union, but we do feel like we are a part of a fraternity because of Art Center. The people that went to Art Center know what you went through, so when you're in the real world, they're there to help you out. It's just a bond you share even after school has ended.

What type of projects are you seeking these days?

As Born has launched our careers, everyone in the collective is each pursuing his own individual freelance careers. Currently, I am freelancing as an Art Director/Director at Motion Theory, a prestigious motion-design firm in Venice, California. We still do work as a collective, but we are not seeking any commercial work at the moment. We are focusing solely on creative content development for our personal narrative-driven ideas, shorts, and artistic projects.

How did the decision to switch to more personal work come about?

I was diagnosed with cancer in 2008, and because of that I had to take a break from working. We had to scale back, and it gave us a moment to focus on what's important. We want to be a less commercial entity, but a content entity. The first thing we did was let go of the space we were renting, because we didn't need to carry that overhead. Plus, we realized that since we love what we do, it didn't exactly matter where we worked. When we had an office space, we'd always talk about the days when we worked in the attic—and how much we loved it there. Now we all work in my dining room.

Born is more creative when we work on content creation or self-initiated projects than when we work on commercial projects. Clients usually want what you've already made. So the stuff we will make on our own will steer the boat for the projects people will want from us later on. And clients respond to people who love their work. ✦

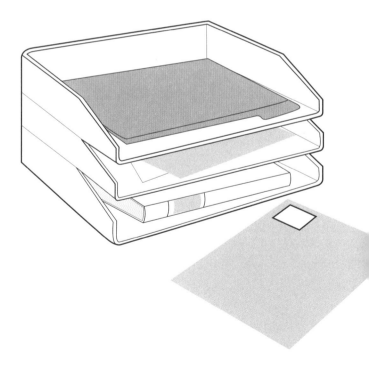

CHAPTER

2

SETTING UP SHOP

Jotting down names for your business. Dreaming of where to set up your studio. The first steps with a freelance career seem almost like child's play. But you'll turn the corner from make-believe to reality once you begin filing paperwork and you realize the weight of the decisions you make. In this chapter we'll outline what you'll need to do to make your freelance career official. We'll walk you through how to establish your business—from picking a freelance name and determining whether to specialize to figuring out your start-up costs and creating a business plan. With this information, you'll be better prepared to open the doors to a successful freelance business.

Picking a Freelance Name

Choosing the right name is very important. It defines you, gives potential clients a taste of your sensibility, and is something that you'll want to stick with as you build your client base. You can either go eponymous (that is, use your own name) or create a new business name. For solo freelancers, the most popular route is to use their given name, because it clearly announces their freelance status. But that option may not be suitable for you, especially if you have a common name, if there's a chance you might expand your business into a multiperson studio, or if you can foresee going through a name change in the future (e.g., through marriage). So if you want more flexibility with your business, it's a good idea to come up with a simple and memorable name that speaks to your target audience. Make sure it's something that can be easily pronounced and is a name that you won't outgrow. Also, take your potential business name out for a test drive. Introduce it to friends and family members to see how they react; you might discover that it comes across differently to others than the way it did in your head.

You'll also need to consider legal aspects when choosing a name—and that applies even if you want to use your given name. First, make sure no other business is already using the name. You'd be surprised how common it is to come up with a name, only to find that it's already being used. And you also have to be careful if you share a surname with any well-known establishments (e.g., your name is Pat Starbucks), because there could be legal ramifications down the road. Check with your county clerk's office, as well as the secretary of state's office, to make sure the name you've chosen isn't already licensed for use or incorporated in your

state. On the federal level, you can check with the U.S. Patent and Trademark Office (USPTO) through a search on their Web site (see Resources) to verify that the name has not been trademarked or service marked. You'll avoid a lot of headaches (and a possible lawsuit) down the line if you do your homework early on.

Specializing vs. Generalizing

As you carve out your freelance career, you have the ultimate power to identify the exact types of jobs you want to work on. Do you want to be a photographer for all seasons, shooting everything from interiors and fashion to dog portraits? Or perhaps you want to be a film producer focusing specifically on documentaries? Or maybe you want to be a niche Web designer and produce only Flash animation? How you define your freelance occupation is up to you—you can be as general or as specific as you want. Ultimately, you should focus on offering the specific set of skills in which you excel and that you enjoy the most—while ensuring that there is a market in need of those skills.

But keep in mind that maximizing your available services doesn't always mean maximizing your client base. In fact, specialists can be highly sought after as experts in a particular area.

Some fields, like graphic design, lend themselves to generalization. Oftentimes clientele come with a broad range of design needs—from logos and packaging to marketing materials and a Web site. The biggest challenge for generalist freelancers is to put together a cohesive portfolio that demonstrates their strengths and personal style across a wide range of subjects. But keep in mind that maximizing your available services doesn't always mean maximizing your client base. In fact, specialists can be highly sought after as experts in a particular area. And the more specialized you become, the less likely you'll be to find competitors offering the same exact service. So whether you've chosen to be a skilled typographer or an à la carte graphic designer, the beauty of freelancing is that your plans can change according to your whims.

Imagine sitting atop a glacier and arranging a set of skis for an Eddie Bauer photo shoot or assembling a seascape within a fish tank for a *Field and Stream* magazine spread. This is a typical workday for Lauren Shields and a far cry from the projects she styled and produced for five years as a craft editor for *Martha Stewart Living*. Ready to show off her own creative point of view, Lauren mustered up the courage to switch to the less-predictable lifestyle of a freelance career. With a Johnny-on-the-spot attitude that's lauded in the publishing and editorial industries, Lauren has earned a strong reputation among big-name clients ranging from editorial to catalog. For Lauren, there's no such thing as a typical workday. One day she's freezing a hunting rifle in ice for *Field and Stream*, the next she's constructing interior design projects for *Better Homes and Gardens*, and the next she's turning empty white walls into an ad-ready statement for Canadian fashion brand Joe Fresh. Given the fact that her freelance career has been going strong since 2005, it's little wonder that Lauren declares it's the best career change she's ever made.

What is actually involved in prop styling?

The particulars of my job are incredibly varied and diverse, depending on the assignment and the client. I frequently joke that *prop stylist* actually translates to "professional shopper and expert schlepper." But there is so much more involved. I am responsible for sourcing, gathering, designing, producing, providing, and arranging all the objects for a particular photo shoot set and building each shot from the ground up. Typically, these are inanimate objects, but sometimes the occasional dog, fish, cat, insect, or bird wrangling is required.

What's your process like for approaching a new job?

When I am assigned a project, the first thing I do is visualize the final photo or product and make a list of all the elements and details that could be part of the image. From here I create a master prop list of everything I'll need to make that shot successful. This includes all sorts of supplies, including surfaces [i.e., paper, wood, or Plexiglas], backgrounds [i.e., painted flats, wallpaper, or BeadBoard], supplies to make the projects, and props to use in the shot [i.e., furniture, tabletop decor, home textiles, lighting, or art for walls]. It takes a lot of research and legwork to hunt down the perfect props and accessories for each assignment and to make certain that you stay on brand, to ensure that each prop is right for the client.

What kind of, and how much, prep work do you do on your own before going into a photo shoot? Do you bill for the prep work?

The prep work is sometimes more involved and demanding than the actual shoot days. Especially if the story is particularly craft heavy, shopping and producing all the details can take weeks, while the shoot may only last two days. For example, I may spend days wrapping hundreds of Christmas presents, while it will only take a few hours to arrange and shoot them. And, yes, the prep days are billed just like shoot days, at the same day rate.

How do you receive client feedback?

Every client is different. Some require preproduction meetings where you literally bring everything in and show photos in advance, so there aren't any surprises. Other clients trust your judgment and creativity and are happy to work out any kinks that day on set. But almost always the decisions are figured out before coming to set. Once I'm on set, I also get feedback from the other creatives at the shoot, such as the photographer and art director, who see the set from a totally different perspective and give suggestions for changes that I may not have thought of on my own. It's wonderful to make things look beautiful, but also equally exciting and challenging to make something ironic, grotesque, or not beautiful.

Do you feel that your location in New York has helped you gain new clients, or could you be doing your job from anywhere?

Being in New York has been absolutely crucial to my career as a prop stylist. This might have been less true when the economy was booming, since the majority of my assignments were in exotic locations outside New York, so I could have flown in from anywhere. But in cases where people need a stylist and they've heard someone mention your name before, being just a subway ride away has been beneficial. Though there is a heavy concentration of stylists in New York, I am a believer that there's enough work to go around.

**How can someone with no background in styling educate him- or
herself in that field? Do you have advice for how one would go about
building a portfolio from scratch?**

It might sound a little corny, but the adage "stop and smell the roses" can
really benefit someone who wants a career in styling. By paying attention to
little vignettes and objects around you, you'll discover unlimited sources of
inspiration. Whether it's how a bakery displays the croissants or the window
merchandising at your favorite store, there's always a lesson about scale,
color, and how objects interact with one another.

The best way to build a portfolio without having any clients is to
experiment around your own home. Test out your propping skills by shifting
things around on your bookcase, mixing and matching your sheets and
blankets, or by using your walls to display all kinds of art. Then take photos
of these styled areas to see what works and what doesn't. You can build a
portfolio with these images by bartering services with photographer friends
who are also looking to build their own portfolios.

**What do you enjoy most about being able to do your work on a free-
lance basis?**

The variety of projects I get to produce is such a thrill to me. I have learned
that I am most productive and inventive in shorter, intense bursts of time
and that reporting to an office or desk every day tends to squash my
creativity and my efficiency. There's also something about photo shoots
that evokes a feeling of summer camp; there is this unique group of people
on location working together creatively, sharing an experience that can
never be replicated. The friends I've made and places I've visited because of
my job have enriched my life in the most incredible way. Being surrounded
by talented people, whether on a seaplane over Vancouver or on the shores
of Hawaii, is just amazing. After that, a cubicle in a high-rise just doesn't
have the same charm.

Where to Work?

For freelancers, the de facto studio is usually their home. When you're start-ing out, the low overhead and convenience of a home-based studio makes for a suitable, economically sensible situation. You can work in your pajamas, grab lunch from the kitchen, and access your work at all hours. Spare bed-rooms, basements, or garages are often good locations. But if your home is low on available square footage, your dining room may have to pinch-hit as a studio for now. No matter where you set up shop, it helps to define bound-aries with doors or room dividers—particularly if you share a place with roommates or your family. Also, if you plan to have clients visit, pay close attention to the appearance and professionalism of your home studio. Once you've turned your home into an effective machine for working, you may even choose to stay there long after you're able to afford an outside studio. But if you don't think that "7245 Peach Blossom Court" carries enough professional heft on your business card, if you get easily distracted at home, or if you need daily interaction with other people, then renting a studio might make more sense. Check out local newspapers, online community boards, and rental Web sites to find places and compare the location, size, and price options. Or consider sharing a studio space with friends or other self-employed creatives. Sharing a space with other artists can make for a motivating, energized workplace, as you can turn to your colleagues for feedback and ideas and even share resources.

DOES THE BIG CITY EQUAL BIG WORK?

Simply stated: big cities usually offer big opportunities. Given their size, big cities have a lot to offer, namely a larger pool of clientele. Certain metropolitan areas are also the hubs of creative industries. New York is home to the majority of the fashion and publishing companies in the United States, while Los Angeles is the center of the entertainment industry. So it makes sense for some freelancers to move to these cities (even for a short while), simply to get a foothold in the business. You can make contacts and attend industry events more easily. You'll also be able to meet your clients in person. And of course, there's a certain cachet that comes with saying "I'm a fashion photographer in New York City." But big city life isn't for everyone. The trade-off is usually a higher cost of living. Which brings us to the pluses of setting up your business in smaller cities. In a smaller city you can be a big fish in a small pond. Clients in smaller cities are often delighted to find talented local freelancers. Unless clients or projects demand regular in-person meetings or assignments, it may not be necessary to live in the same city as your clients. With the Internet and video conference calls, clients are becoming more acclimated to the idea of working with creatives they've never met in person.

Financing Your First Year

The good news about freelancing is that you don't need a whole lot of capital to get started. Overhead is usually low, especially if you're working from home. Still, until your freelance business turns a profit, you'll need to find a way to pay your bills. Indeed, most business consultants recommend saving a year's worth of living expenses before starting a business. That seems like a lot, but it's certainly doable. To figure out what it costs for you to live for one year, calculate all of your major and minor expenses. Don't forget to include daily expenses you may overlook, like bottled water or cab fares—these things add up. If you find that the balance of your existing savings account doesn't match a year's worth of living expenses, or that your capital is tied up in your shoe collection, you may want to make some lifestyle changes. Consider getting a roommate, moving to a less-expensive part of town, or asking your partner or spouse to pay the majority of the bills until you can contribute part of your earnings.

For the first year, it's important to be aware that your earnings might not match your hours of labor. So you'll want to be conservative in your business spending.

You can certainly use credit cards to help finance some start-up costs, but use them wisely! With credit cards, you may encounter hidden fees that jack up your monthly payments, and, if you're not careful, you may find yourself suffering from the all-too-common curse of credit card debt. Look for small-business credit cards with low annual percentage rates, as well as those that offer cash back or reward options. Make sure to read the fine print of every option, and do your best to pay the balance every month, so you don't find yourself overspent with excessive debt. Also, look into capital in the form of grants and prizes, especially if yours is a woman- or minority-owned business. Check out local business incubators that give support and guidance to small businesses, economic development centers, and small-business development centers for information on grants that are available in your area. You can start with the U.S. Small Business Administration's Web Site (see Resources) which will provide more information on small business groups (like SCORE and Small Business Development Centers).

For the first year, it's important to be aware that your earnings might not match your hours of labor. So you'll want to be conservative in your business spending. Buy equipment and supplies as needed, rather than committing limited funds to purchasing everything at once. Avoid getting an outside studio space if you can swing a work-at-home situation comfortably. And consider bartering—maybe you can work out a deal where you'll photograph family portraits in exchange for getting someone to program your Web site. In time, your business will turn a livable profit and will bring in enough to support your present and future business expenses. When that day comes, you'll have the joy of knowing that your smart and frugal decisions paid off.

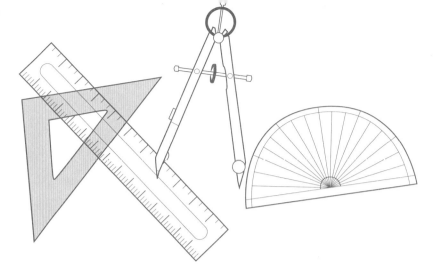

Studio Tools and Equipment

Having a well-equipped, well-organized, and inspiring studio is essential to being a productive and effective freelancer. Pay attention to ergonomics with your chair and workstations, especially if you'll be spending hours at a computer. Put up a large corkboard or clothesline to display clippings, images, and swatches as inspiration for upcoming projects. When you're juggling multiple projects, keep a calendar updated with your daily, weekly, and monthly schedule. Your calendar is an indispensable tool for keeping track of deadlines and providing estimates for deliverables. In addition, it's helpful to use time-tracking software (see Resources) that registers every minute you spend on each project, so you can properly bill your clients. Especially with flat-fee projects, this software can also help you figure out if you have indeed earned a fair amount for the time spent.

Up-to-date equipment, including hardware and software, is great for your small business arsenal, but technology doesn't come cheap. In the beginning you'll need to be prudent with your purchases. In general, pick equipment that will increase your productivity and help your bottom line. Ask yourself, "Do I really need this? How will it help my business?" If you want to buy it just because it looks cool, reconsider. It's helpful to make a complete list of needs categorized by "what I need now," "what I'll need soon," and "what I can wait on." When possible, look into cost-effective options for renting, sharing, or purchasing refurbished equipment.

Art school students take note: look to the right and left of you, because your future business partners could be sitting alongside you. In 2002, graphic designer Jenny Volvovski, animator Matt Lamothe, and illustrator Julia Rothman graduated from the Rhode Island School of Design. While Jenny and Matt began their postgraduate lives working at a media agency and an events company (respectively), Julia began doing freelance illustration work for *Teen People* magazine. When a client approached Julia to create a Web site for a dog clothing company, she called on Jenny and Matt to help with programming and animation. When this serendipitous collaboration proved successful, it cemented their idea to join forces despite the distance between them, with Julia in Brooklyn and Matt and Jenny in Chicago. Since 2006, their work has caught the eye of clients ranging from academic institutions (Columbia University) to indie design bloggers (Design*Sponge). In 2008 they won the prestigious Young Guns Award from the Art Directors Club, which recognizes breakthrough creative talent under thirty, firmly establishing their status as the dream team of the Web design world.

How did the name Also come about?

Matt: When thinking about names, we wanted an all-inclusive name that incorporated everything we did or could possibly do in the future and wasn't hindered by any specific format or type of work. It came to us one day while walking down the street, brainstorming names. As soon as we said the word also out loud, Julia literally started screaming! We love the name, because we imagine expanding the brand into other businesses like an Also Store or Also Furniture. However, once we finally chose a name, we decided that the name didn't have to be the "be all and end all" of our business, but that we would define our company from there on out with the quality of our work.

Tell us about your work process for each client job and how you divide up the work.

Julia: From the very beginning, we have tried to maximize each person's skills and strengths. In addition to illustration, I really enjoy networking, so I handle all of our marketing. Matt creates all the animation and does the initial research for all jobs. And Jenny handles graphic and Web design as well as the estimating and project management, because she's super organized. For every project, regardless of how much or little each person's area of expertise is needed, we all discuss concepts together and serve as co–art directors, overseeing the process from beginning to end.

How many projects do you work on at one time?

Jenny: We typically work on ten projects at one time. Some jobs are really quick, and some take over a year from start to finish, so we always have a range of projects going on at different stages of completion. At this point, we have started scheduling new client projects in advance. This helps us to establish our work schedule over the next several months while giving us time to finish up the current jobs on our plate, so that we never bite off more than we can chew.

How often do you get together via video conference?

Julia: We actually leave our video chat on all day long, which makes it feel like we're all in a real office together. Jenny and Matt can hear my dog, Rudy, barking in the background while we bounce ideas off each other throughout the day. It feels less like we're working separately, because we can freely talk to one another whenever we want, or we can go for hours at a time without saying a word. Our video chat setup has been crucial for our company. It allows us to interact more freely, since we can not only talk but also show each other sketches or concepts we're working on and receive instant feedback.

Do you ever meet your clients in person, or do you find most interaction with clients to be virtual?

Jenny: We prefer to meet a client at least once, if possible. We like to connect with them in person to get a better sense of their personality and work style so that we'll be better equipped to effectively communicate with them via e-mail or on the phone after that. Obviously, you can't always meet with a client if they are far away, but if you have the option, in-person meetings can help lead to better working relationships down the road.

How did you determine how much to charge?

Jenny: In the beginning, we really didn't know how much to charge, and we did a lot of guessing on our fees and in estimating how much time we'd spend on a project. We actually had an unexpected reality check one day when there was a plumber doing work in our apartment who was charging more per hour than we were! That's when we realized we could charge much more for our services. As we got busier, we learned what people were willing to pay and what our work was worth, so we gradually ramped up our pricing. While we did undercharge initially, it did allow us to get more work and build our portfolio, so it's not always a bad thing to offer lower rates when starting out. Our suggestion when you're new to freelancing is to charge the amount you honestly feel you should get, and the client will tell you if it's too much. That way, at least you have a starting point, and you can decide to negotiate further with the client or not.

How can a freelancer find interesting work?

Matt: Don't be afraid to approach people you admire and want to work with. You can write a simple, genuine e-mail to a company expressing your interest. An e-mail gives you a bit of anonymity and makes it easier to approach someone in a less forceful way than cold-calling or soliciting face-to-face. Sure, some people may not respond to your letter, but a surprising amount of people will. For example, we loved the shop Reform School in Los Angeles and noticed they didn't have an e-commerce site. So we wrote to them telling them how much we enjoy what they do and that we'd like to work with them if they were ever interested in e-commerce. They happened to be looking for someone to design their online site, so our cold e-mailing worked out!

Also, if there are slow periods, we take advantage of that time to work on fun things that we've always wanted to work on but don't usually have time for. These self-created projects give us an outlet from our normal client work and open our eyes to other types of projects we might want to work on. Lulls in business are also a good time to be proactive and get new and different types of clients that you have always wanted [to work with]. Sometimes when you're busy, it's easy to let the clients come to you. But oftentimes when you're not actively seeking new clients, you end up doing a lot of the same work for the same types of clients. So take the time to reach out and find new clients who do things you haven't done before but would love to do.

What advice do you have for freelancers wanting to join forces with other creatives? What are some musts and some things to avoid doing?
Julia: Before you decide to start a company with other creatives, work on some projects together to make sure you can in fact work well together. There is no need to jump right into a company, so you can start by joining forces as individual freelancers and take it one project at a time. You also want to work with people who have different skills that complement your own. Since we each do different things, we're able to individually take ownership of our particular skill set. Don't let friendship be the deciding factor, as friends don't always make the best partners. In the end, you have to work with people you respect and whose opinions you trust. Finally, our ultimate test to see if you're team worthy is to go on a road trip together and make sure you can stand being with the other person [or people] for more than forty-eight hours! ⸺

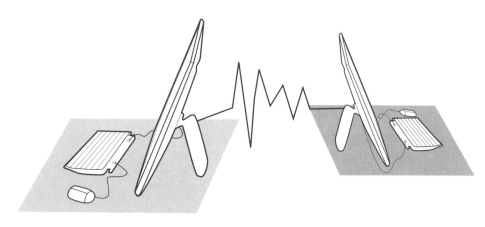

Finding Vendors

When you're producing a project, you'll often feel like a general contractor: sometimes you have to assemble a team of people to get the job done. So it helps to have a stable of vendors to call on, especially when you're in a crunch: local quick-print shops, commercial printers, service bureaus, binderies, or film scanners, to name a few. When you're new, you'll have to gather information on potential vendors from scratch. Get in the habit of

To get the best quotes, familiarize yourself with vendor terminology.

accumulating contacts as you come across them through the yellow pages, online searches, networking, friends, family, and peers. Hold on to cards for services or companies you may need in the future, because you never know when you'll need a sewn-stitch binder or a computer metal control mill. To get the best quotes, familiarize yourself with vendor terminology. If you approach a printer who asks "Are there any bleeds in your file?" or "At what resolution do you want your negatives scanned?" you should know the answer to these questions. If you don't, you're bound to sound like an amateur, which may result in higher quotes. Also, when contacting new vendors, ask for general information about their range of services and sample pricing for a potential job. Keep records of the information and estimates you receive. Take note of the capabilities and equipment of each vendor, as well as who can work under rushed time constraints, whose sales reps you felt most comfortable talking to, and who has the best value for the services provided. Once you start working with vendors you trust, you will find they can also be great resources for finding others in the business—so be sure to ask for recommendations.

Making It Official

As soon as you offer your creative services for a profit, you're considered a business. You will be subject to taxes, rules, laws, and regulations concerning your business and will have to apply for a variety of licenses and permits. You will also have to consider protective measures such as health and liability insurance. This all may sound scary and bureaucratic, but, once you break it down into steps, it's not so difficult. Here are the basic necessities for starting your freelance business:

Business license

Depending on your city and state, you may be required to apply for a license to conduct business. Check with your local chamber of commerce to find out what type of license you'll need, how to go about applying for it, and what fees are involved. You usually have to pay a nominal fee for the license, which you'll then need to renew yearly. This license needs to be displayed in your work space.

Zoning

Before you can start a business, whether it's in your home or at an outside studio, you'll have to check with your city planning division to see if zoning allows businesses at that location. Many cities do allow home-based businesses, as long as the home is used primarily as a residence and your business activities do not affect your neighbors. Luckily, most freelance pursuits do not create much noise or disturbance, so zoning issues are rare.

Fictitious business name

Unless you're using your legal name, you'll need to register a fictitious business name, also known as a DBA (Doing Business As). This is usually done through your county clerk's office (some states require registration through the secretary of state) as fictitious business names must be unique per state or county (i.e., two businesses in the same area cannot use the same fictitious name). You'll be required to register the name with the county or state and publish a notice in your local newspaper; you'll then submit an affidavit to either the county or the state to show that you have fulfilled the publication requirement. Most local newspapers are familiar with this process (for some small newspapers, these ads are a regular source of revenue), and their ad sales representatives can walk you through it should you have any questions. After you register the name, oftentimes you'll get a solicitation from several papers offering to run your ad, and some will send the affidavit to the county clerk on your behalf. This is an important step; otherwise, conducting business under a name other than your legal name may be considered fraud.

Service mark

Similar to a trademark for products, a service mark is a distinctive name, sign, symbol, device, or any combination of those, used to identify and distinguish your services from those of others. Though it is not necessary to service mark your business, it adds a level of protection against future businesses that may try to infringe upon your business name or brand. To register a service mark (which covers the whole United States and not just your area), you have to go through the U.S. Patent and Trademark Office (see Resources) to do a search. If the name you've chosen is available, you'll file an application for use of the service mark. This process can take any-where from a few months to more than a year, depending on the basis for filing and any legal issues that could arise. Usually delays occur if a service mark already exists that has a name and/or type of service similar to yours. A small-business lawyer can take care of the process for you.

Business bank account

For tax purposes, any money spent or income earned with your business cannot be commingled with personal finances, so it's important to open a business bank account. You'll have to show the bank your fictitious name statement, along with your business license. It's also a good idea to open a savings account where you deposit a portion of your income, so come tax time you won't find yourself scrounging around to make tax payments.

Federal tax ID

You will need to file for a federal tax ID number, also known as an employer ID number (EIN), if your freelance venture is a partnership or if you're a sole proprietor with employees. Otherwise, as a solo freelancer, your individual social security number is sufficient for filing taxes. It is also worth considering filing for an EIN if you feel uncomfortable giving your social security number to every client who requires you to fill out a W-9 form. (The W-9 is a request for a taxpayer identification number, which is often required before a client can pay you.) You can familiarize yourself with the paperwork, rules, and regulations through IRS publications. On its Web site (see Resources), the IRS offers downloadable PDFs specifically for small businesses and self employed individuals.

Your legal structure

Most freelancers automatically choose their legal structure as a sole proprietorship. However, there are tax and asset protection benefits (in case you are sued) if you register your business as another legal structure, such as a limited liability corporation (LLC), S-corporation, or C-corporation. Visit the Small Business Administration Web site (see Resources) to read more about the various types of legal structures, or consult with an accountant or lawyer to see what's best for you.

Liability insurance

Your homeowner's or renter's insurance typically covers only a small portion of your home office, so you may need to request additional work-at-home liability coverage, especially if there is any possibility of someone being injured while in your home office. If clients visit your studio or an intern comes a few times a week, you need to make sure you're covered should any mishap occur. Alternatively, you can arrange for a separate business liability insurance policy. Consult an insurance broker to find the insurance policy that is best for your company.

Health insurance

It goes without saying that health insurance is incredibly important. There are many health coverage plans, so it shouldn't be difficult to find one that serves your needs and budget. Contact insurance companies in your state to find out the costs of coverage for individual insurance. If you have a spouse or domestic partner who is covered by his or her employer, consider getting added to that health insurance policy. Your last employer may also offer a COBRA (Consolidated Omnibus Budget Reconciliation Act) plan, which extends the coverage you had at that job. You can also join guilds and unions, such as the Directors Guild of America or the Freelancers Union, which provide health care options for freelancers in their respective industries.

Domain name

Once you have your business name in the clear, search online to see if a domain name is available. First-choice Web site URLs are becoming increasingly harder to secure, so it's a good idea to buy your domain name as quickly as possible (see Resources). If your first-choice domain name is already taken, consider alternative descriptors or words that can be attached without making the domain name too complicated. The key is to come up with a domain name that's easily searchable. Once you have the domain name, redirect it to your temporary Web site or create a placeholder while your Web site is in the works.

Phone line

If you are working from home, you'll have to establish a separate phone line for your business, because legally you can't print your home number as your business number on any of your business materials. A cell phone might be an even more sensible option, especially for freelancers who do most of their work on location and outside their office.

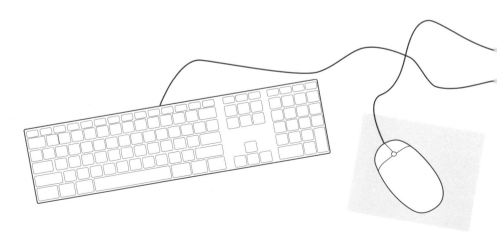

Creating a Business Plan

A business plan is key to your success. Unfortunately, writing one is a step often overlooked by freelancers. It is basically a written outline describing your business and evaluating its financial viability. A business plan is an effective tool to help you set goals and determine what you need, both logistically and financially, to run your freelance operation successfully. A business plan is also necessary if you need to secure loans from banks and investors and is helpful to have when asking for constructive feedback from mentors in your field.

THE FIVE MAIN PARTS OF A TRADITIONAL BUSINESS PLAN ARE:

01 **A mission statement,** which consists of a statement or group of statements outlining your motivations, values, and goals for your freelance venture.

02 **Background information,** which provides the facts about your company and the people involved in it. When was your business legally established? Who is part of your business, and what skills or services does each person contribute?

03 **A list of services,** which describes in detail which services you are offering. Focus on the specialized set of skills you intend to offer initially and discuss the end result—what you hope to accomplish with your services.

04 **A marketing analysis,** which asks questions such as: What makes you stand out from the competition? Who is your target client market, what are the clients' needs, and where are your potential clients located? How will you reach potential clients and promote your services?

05 **Financial projections,** which will include your monthly and one-year projections of your profits, expenses, and cash flow and an overall analysis of how and when you'll become financially profitable. These numbers will help you assess if you have enough of your own capital to start the business or if you need to look into a bank loan or support from investors.

It's important that your business plan be realistic. Don't downplay your potential weaknesses or forecast windfall profits. Of course, it can be difficult to project revenue when you don't have any previous numbers to rely on. Set financial goals that are attractive enough to keep you motivated, but also realistic enough that they are within reach. As with any estimation, you will find that the reality may be different. You can adjust your projections as you gain more financial knowledge about your business.

A business plan should also be versatile, to accommodate any number of potential scenarios that could arise when you start your business. Deal with best- and worst-case scenarios: What if your career is an overnight success? What will you do to handle the volume? What is your plan for the slow times? Keep in mind that your business plan doesn't have to be a lengthy novel. If the format of a traditional business plan is unappealing to you, simply create a set of financial and creative goals on a monthly basis. Either way, you need to have some sort of plan laid out for your business. And remember that a business plan is meant to be flexible, an ever-evolving tool that you can add to and revise as your business grows.

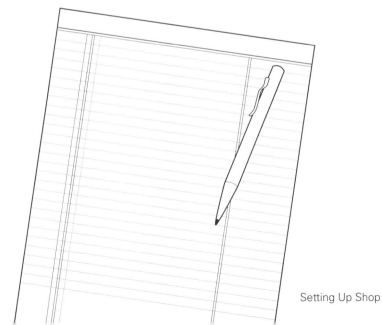

GETTING THE WORD OUT

CHAPTER

3

As much as we'd love for it to be the case, clients won't just come knocking as soon as you open for business. In order for potential buyers to find you, they have to first know you exist and then see evidence of your talent at work. So announce to the world, through industry blogs or postcards to potential clients, that you've arrived on the scene. But beware of the pitfall of putting your best efforts only into primping for the coming-out party then relying on your work to generate interest thereafter. A successful freelancer continually sends out mailers, revises his portfolio, and follows up with his client base. Making marketing an integral part of your business will guarantee that you'll have work in six months, twelve months, and even two years down the road. Self-promotion also allows you to exercise a level of control over the types of jobs you attract. This chapter will help you develop strategies to strengthen your portfolio, get your foot in the door with new clients, maintain a steady client base, and raise your profile in the creative world. You'll gain knowledge to keep you from vanishing into the freelance woodwork, and you'll discover that tooting your own horn can be a fun and imaginative pursuit.

Establishing Your Brand

J.Crew is about classic American style. BMW is about high-performance luxury. Braun is about clean, functional design. How would you like people to describe your company? Like the companies mentioned here, yours should evoke a belief system with a central idea or key attribute that characterizes your business. Branding, in many ways, is like bestowing a personality on your company. Write down the qualities you think your brand should embody: Is the feel of your business whimsical or serious? Is it luxurious and sleek or crafty and homespun? Your company's personality should fit your work, but it doesn't necessarily need to be a replica of its owner. To help define what your company should be, check out your competitors, as well as companies that share your aesthetic. Pay attention to what inspires you while making it a point to never copy. The key is to respect and analyze your competitors—take note of what they're doing and use it as an opportunity to capitalize on doing something different. Remember, your brand should express your unique point of view, style, and vision; it should be relevant to your target market; and above all, it should be memorable and recognizable.

Branding is about projecting positive impressions of your company to your target market. Every detail connected to the operation of your business, from the typeface on your Web site all the way down to how you answer the phone, has to be in line with your brand. As you create your brand identity, make sure you consider these three main components:

01 Design: your logo, business card, letterhead, Web site, colors, typefaces, and any graphics used to visually communicate what your business is about.

02 Communications and marketing: all your visual and verbal messages, including advertising, public relations, and any promotional tools used to get new jobs or attract clients; establish who your target market is, so you know that you are properly communicating to it.

03 Behavior: the manner in which you conduct your business—from the goals and mission statement set forth in your business plan, to your interaction with clients, to your reputation—all should fit your brand.

Branding is an all-encompassing experience. That said, effective branding is not about slapping a logo or slogan onto everything you do. When something appears overly self-promotional and sales driven, it turns people away rather than bringing them in. Instead, create a brand with a certain mystique that attracts people to you. The trick to branding is subtlety. Your business card, letterhead, Web site, and studio walls don't need to look like they all were cut from the same polka-dot pattern. Avoid being too matchy-matchy: leave room for surprise. Remember that you can evoke the qualities of your brand through different materials and methods. Harnessing the power of branding can almost be like devising a secret recipe—you might not get the portions or ingredients right the first time, but once you do, you'll find branding to be a powerful tool that gives you control over how your audience perceives you.

DESIGNING A LOGO

Designed to be instantly recognized, logos are powerful symbols. Creating a successful logo often takes experience, but, curiously, some creatives decide to tackle this job on their own, without any logo-design know-how. Skip the crash course in Illustrator (and the amateur logo that would surely ensue) and find a specialist instead. Logos don't come cheap, but with a bit of research you'll be able to find an experienced designer who will work within your budget or, better yet, be willing to barter for your services.

Welcome Exposure

How will people know what you do and what your abilities are? People won't always recognize your abilities on their own. Every day, a better candidate is turned down for a promotion, but did this guy make his abilities known to his boss? Probably not. Likewise, it will be your job to display your worth. Remember, it's not your client's job to figure it out.

As a freelancer, you'll have many avenues for showing off your talents. All of the promotional materials you create, including your portfolio, Web site, and business stationery, are the most obvious self-promotional tools. They should also serve to underscore your brand and showcase your creative skills. As you create these items, know that clients will judge everything that comes out of your office on its appearance. Since you are a visual auteur, presentation is everything. Keep in mind that your look should be about your business's personality and your work, not your wallet. And it's not just about looks alone; how you present yourself verbally both on paper (in your correspondence) and in person (when you're networking) is a part of the total package.

The Portfolio

In the creative world, it's all about the portfolio. Obviously, your body of work will be your most important asset. A good portfolio showcases your creativity, talent, range, ambition, professionalism, insight, and passion—along with a consistent aesthetic. There's no exact number of pieces you should show in your portfolio, but we suggest starting with eight to twelve. You may need more, depending on your field (with photography, you'll likely need at least twenty images), but the key is to show enough examples high-lighting your capabilities without overwhelming your viewer with too many pieces, being too repetitive, or showing work that is no longer relevant to what you do.

Your portfolio should include a combination of the work you have successfully completed, work that reflects your signature style, and the type of work you want to do in the future. Include only the strongest pieces in your portfolio, ones that showcase your style or capabilities, and always display the type of work you're looking to do. For instance, if you're a film editor, your portfolio (or reel) should be composed of short clips demonstrating your technical abilities (e.g., fast cuts, interesting transitions) rather than complete scenes. And keep in mind that order matters: organize the pieces of your portfolio like you would a good book; start and end with the strongest pieces, and compose a balanced and cohesive story with the remaining visuals in between.

Here's a look at the specific elements that could be included in your portfolio:

Professional work

It's ideal to incorporate completed work done for past employers or pieces commissioned by real, live clients. This work will show your skills in the marketplace and will add relevance and professionalism to your credentials. If you are showing work you've completed for previous employers, get their consent before putting any collective work in your portfolio. It's also important to be honest about authorship and give credit where it is due.

Process and sketches

To give your client a better sense of your thought process, ability to sketch ideas, and skills at translating vague concepts into cohesive visual solutions, highlight at least one project in more detail, from concept to production.

Self-initiated projects

If the work you've done thus far doesn't reflect your current voice and style, or if you want to create a portfolio that is more about who you've become than who you've been, it makes sense to include self-initiated projects. These projects should set the bar for the type of paid work you're looking to do. For example, if you want to branch out into travel photography, document your trip to Greece and include those images in your portfolio.

Student work

If you graduated from college nine years ago, it's probably best to refrain from including any of your student work. Include school assignments in your portfolio only if you are a recent graduate and have not yet completed any other professional work. Over time, you should weed out the samples from your heyday as a student.

Written explanations

For times when you're unable to meet a client in person, it's helpful to supply brief written explanations that provide further insight into each piece. Well-written descriptions can also demonstrate your intelligence, your attention to detail, and the rigor of your work. It's most important to relay who the client was and what the purpose of the job was. Be brief and stay away from sounding overly sales driven. You don't want to overshadow the work with a long, drawn-out description.

Presentation and casing

A portfolio should always be easy to open and view. Although a very large portfolio may offer the space to show your work in all its glory, it would behoove you to have one that actually fits atop a café table, should you meet a client at a coffee shop. You can present work samples separately on individual boards or bind them into a book format. Either way, the portfolio should be clean and clutter-free and able to protect your work from fingerprints or a spilled latte. Make sure all your printouts are printed on substantial paper with a high-quality ink-jet or laser printer.

With all these elements, you may be tempted to include everything you've ever done to show your range of talents. But instead of looking experienced, you might come off looking like you lack focus. When you do have such a breadth of work, you may need to create different portfolios, each one showcasing a different area of your expertise. But you don't need to show all your books to a client—just the one that applies to her specifically. For example, if you're a photographer who shoots both fashion editorials and still-life products, bring only the fashion portfolio when you meet with an editor at *Elle*. If putting together more than one book is too big a hit on your pocketbook, devise a flexible book that allows you to swap out pages to customize it to any potential client's needs.

Assembling a portfolio can be a heavy task. If you find it hard to be objective about your work or struggle with portfolio-inadequacy issues, know that this is normal. Every creative, even the ones who don't like to admit it, experience these feelings on some level. If it has been a while since you've updated your portfolio or you simply need another set of eyes, ask creative peers and mentors for suggestions to make your book stronger. A portfolio is a snapshot of your creative talents at a particular moment. Creatives should always be developing new work, so your portfolio can be current only up to the moment you create it. Assemble your portfolio with enthusiasm tempered by the knowledge that it will change in the future.

Your Web Site

Your Web site will be your hardest-working marketing tool. It rarely takes a day off. It works while you sleep and while you're on vacation. It's always out there, showing off your talent, making connections, and wooing clients near and far. Giving this workhorse a short and simple domain name is a good first step. And, unless you have some HTML or Flash skills at your disposal, you may need to hire a Web designer to create your site. A less-expensive alternative would be to learn how to use Web-site design programs like Dreamweaver. But if you need to get a Web site up quickly and don't have the time or budget to build one from the ground up, use one of many online creative-job sites that provide templates for you for a nominal fee, along with your own URL, so you can post your résumé, portfolio, or samples of your work (see Resources). Clients often check these sites and post job opportunities when looking for qualified freelancers.

As you design your Web site, forget the Flash intro with animated acrobatics spelling out your name. Visitors new to an online portfolio are more interested in a site that loads quickly, presents clear and large images, and has an easy-to-understand navigational system. A site with all the bells and whistles doesn't necessarily make a better impression than a simple one that really highlights your work. It's also good to keep in mind that search engines and blogs can direct people to any page on your site. Since the point of entry may vary, make sure your overall menu, including contact and company information, is easy to find and accessible from every page. We may be stating the obvious, but you'd be surprised at how many Web sites make it difficult to find contact information. Remember that clients are busy and may stick around for only three to five clicks on your site—so help them to get to the information they need quickly, with the least amount of confusion.

Your Web site is more than just an online version of your physical portfolio. It provides more opportunities to show dimensions of your work and your business personality. In your bio, include the requisite background information such as your education, past employers, and the type of work you enjoy. Providing a list of notable clients you've worked with and any press coverage you've earned will serve as an endorsement of your work. But you should also bring a more personal angle to your site by including some fun tidbits, such as links to Web sites and blogs you frequently visit. When people get a sense of who you are and the things you enjoy, it helps them to connect with you on a personal level. And, as your Web site is often the first point of contact for clients, it should consequently be kept up to date. Potential clients expect Web sites to reflect recent work, so update your online portfolio with your latest photographs, sketches, or projects as often as possible.

Good things take time, and there is nothing rushed about Thayer Allyson Gowdy's fifteen-year career. Despite leaving photography school a year shy of graduation, Thayer has, over the years, photographed more than 150 weddings, twenty magazine covers, and twenty books, and she has worked for clients such as Sony, Gymboree, and TRESemmé. With a résumé like that, you'd think she's reached a point in her career where she can rest. But akin to the philosophy that muscles atrophy when you don't use them, for Thayer, creativity can go slack if she doesn't keep it active. So she refuses to rest. In fact, she's just beginning. Attracting clients with her production know-how and outgoing personality, Thayer and her story underscore the truism that freelancing isn't built on talent alone. Her freelance career is testament to what happens when you put a premium on your most important asset: yourself.

Did you work for any companies full-time before freelancing?

I wanted to learn every aspect of the film and photography business, so I took a job as a production assistant in Los Angeles. During shoots, I would be a fly on the wall so I could learn what commercial film and photography producers do. After that job, I became a full-time producer and studio manager for three more years, and I did a bit of location scouting as well. Although I did these things, I always knew I wanted to be a commercial photographer. Working as a producer got my feet wet in the business, and it helped me understand things like making estimates. It made me feel much more secure before going out on my own.

When did you start freelancing?

I actually got my start in weddings. In 1994, I photographed my old roommate's wedding in Paris. Back then, though, wedding photographers weren't as respected as they are now in the industry, so I didn't want to like it. But I did! It's more common now, but not many people were taking an editorial approach to wedding images back then. Suddenly, through word of mouth, I started shooting more weddings. I would work as a producer on weekdays and as a freelance photographer shooting weddings on weekends. Because I worked in the film industry, I got to shoot these really amazing creative weddings of people in the business. I quickly became one of the top wedding photographers in the country. I was doing about fifty weddings a year, so I was booked practically every weekend. I was so busy, I had to quit my job as a producer.

How did you get your first editorial assignment?

Luckily, being a producer, I knew how to sell my work. I knew enough about the industry to take it to another level and get my wedding images in magazines, like *Martha Stewart Weddings*. Soon, editors at *Martha Stewart* started approaching me to buy my existing imagery as stock photography. It was great additional income. But after they bought my imagery for four years, I told them that I could no longer fill their stock requirements. I had formed great relationships with editors there, and I told them that I wanted to be hired for a shoot instead. I think they were initially a little skeptical, because they normally hired a commercial photographer, not a wedding photographer, for editorial shoots. But they eventually gave me a little assignment. Later, a bunch of my contacts left *Martha Stewart* and went to *Real Simple*. When they moved, they started giving me assignments at that magazine. Those were some of the best assignments I've ever received. Shooting for *Real Simple* started to define the look of my work. They were wholly responsible for launching my editorial career.

With commercial editorial shoots, the shoots tend to go over budget, and magazines can lose money. But because of my background in production, I could organize a whole crew without thinking too much—and, more important, without going over budget. I never felt like editors chose me necessarily because of my images, as I honestly didn't feel like my photography was really that unique. There were easily five other photographers they could've chosen. I believed it was my personality and my production capabilities that editors really responded to.

When did you decide to get an agent?

It started with *PDN* [*Photo District News*] magazine. It's pretty much the bible for photographers, and everyone in the industry reads it. Every year they choose thirty photographers internationally that are the top, up-and-coming stars. In 2004, I got a call from *PDN* telling me I was going to be in the *PDN 30* the following year! So before the issue came out, I redid my Web site, organized my portfolios, and decided to get an agent. I knew that coming out in *PDN* would give me more leverage to get an agent. I flew to New York to talk with agents, and I signed with the Clare Agency. Although I had been quite successful without an agent, I wanted to get advertising jobs. And agents do give you a sense of legitimacy.

How do advertising jobs differ from editorial jobs?

With editorials, you're usually booked on the spot. With advertising, you are competing with other photographers who all want to win the same job. It's brutal, but the budgets are huge. Advertising agencies give you the scope of what they're looking for on behalf of their end client. You have to create a proposal and an estimated budget. Your proposal needs to provide the parameters of the project, including where you would shoot it and how much talent (like models and a stylist) you would need to hire. You also have to provide an outline of how you're going to make it all happen. In your proposal, you have to make smart choices—it could make or break the job. Again, my production and location-scouting background has been a great foundation for this type of work. And although advertising jobs are financially fulfilling, the images are usually not as fulfilling as editorial jobs. Advertising is about selling a product, not conveying an idea. It would be great to get an advertising gig with a great visionary art director.

What is a typical advertising budget like?

It could be anywhere from $2,500 per shoot day to upwards of a $100,000 per day. With ranges like this, it's helpful to have an agent. Artists tend to underbid themselves, because they don't think they are as valuable as they are. But agents have no apprehension—they know how much you and a project are worth. I might think the budget for an ad job might be only $5,000 a day, where as my agent thinks it's $20,000 a day.

What advice do you have for putting together a portfolio?

As a commercial photographer, you have to shoot what you love, because you'll get jobs based on that. What you have in your portfolio will define your career path. If you don't want to be stuck doing something you don't want to do, don't show it in your portfolio. When you put your portfolio together, focus on continuity, quality, and clear vision. Don't put together a book that is all over the place, or a client or agent won't know what to do with you. If you have a big mishmash of beautiful landscapes and then, in contrast, indie portraits that look straight out of *Nylon* magazine in the same book, don't sit around wondering why you weren't hired for a job. You have to make a book that is personal. Make your style loud and clear! Clients want to be inspired. In the beginning, you can start off with two different books. Right now, I have several portfolios: lifestyle (my main one), portraits, beauty, and kids. There are about twenty-five to thirty-five images in each portfolio. I just send the book that pertains to the client. I have a duplicate of each book, just in case I go to a meeting and they need to borrow it. It's always good to have a spare copy. If you only have one portfolio, then you should give a leave-behind, like a postcard. You need to leave an image with them so they can put it on their wall to remember you. One thing to note is that your online portfolio and physical book should match. If a client loved a picture on your Web site, they will look for it in your book. They may choose you for a project based on a single image they loved.

Do you do any promotional activity for your work?

When I was with the Clare Agency, they did about six different promotions in a year that go out to about 3,000 people, most of whom are photo editors and art directors. My agent also put together a massive book with all her photographers. In general, I spend anywhere from $50,000 to $75,000 per year on promotion, which includes designing and producing my portfolios, maintaining my Web site, sending out mailers, and travel costs for in-person meetings. Every year, I make it a point to visit Minneapolis, Chicago, and New York to meet with photo editors, magazine publishing houses, and ad agencies. You have to be super proactive in this business. Grab your portfolio and get on a plane and go! It's the act of meeting people that will make your career. If they put a face, personality, and conversation to a name, it helps to form a relationship. For me, I put a value on my personality. People want to hire me because of me. So make an impression and sell yourself.

Business Stationery

Don't underestimate the power of paper. Your business stationery, including letterhead, business cards, and brochures, can make a sizable visual impact on a potential client, so send notes on your letterhead at all times. And create smaller representations of your portfolio as a leave-behind, such as a postcard or sample booklet, so you can give them to a client at the end of a meeting. Make sure to always carry your business cards with you, because you never know who you'll meet. Despite its diminutive size, a business card is the most vital piece of your business stationery. Along with your logo, the card should simply and clearly state your contact information and Web address. Avoid trying to list all your services, because that will only distract from the card's overall message. Your card should convey just enough information to attract a client's interest, convey an idea of what you do, and incite curiosity to make a client want to find out more about you.

Publicity

Wouldn't it be great to open up the pages of your favorite trade glossy and see accolades of your work staring back at you? Indeed, getting a press mention is one way to raise your profile and awareness of your brand.

Editors are always on the lookout for fresh faces and fresh ideas, so do your research and find out which magazines and periodicals are the best fit.

Look for opportunities to get featured in the press, whether through industry or trade press or general mass-market publications. Editors are always on the lookout for fresh faces and fresh ideas, so do your research and find out which magazines and periodicals are the best fit. The article you pitch doesn't necessarily have to focus solely on your own work. Think about different angles to pitch: a poster you illustrated for a charitable organization might be right for a design magazine; a pitch about your cool workspace befits a lifestyle magazine. Or, if your work consists of a nontraditional business model, contact a business magazine to see if it will profile you. After coming up with a focus for your pitch, send editors images and a short description of your project or pitch idea. Publications want exclusivity, so be sure to send story ideas to one magazine at a time starting with the one you want the most. Once you establish a relationship with a publication, you may be approached in the future for quotes or to comment on articles. You may even be asked to write articles as an expert in your field. A note to the wise, however: seeing your face or work gracing the pages of your favorite magazine is a thrill and a great endorsement for your business, but remember that getting a press mention does not guarantee instant success.

Blogging

These days, everyone seems to be a blogger—and that isn't a bad thing. As a creative businessperson, you can make the Internet's quick pace work to your advantage. A blog can become an important marketing tool, because it offers readers a more personal look into your world. You should definitely post about your most recent work and what inspires you, photo outtakes that missed the final cut for a job, or sketches that show your process as you work on your next graphic novel. If your potential clients read your blog, they'll quickly gain insight on your personality and talents and will see what skills you possess. But be careful of getting overly self-promotional; the faintest whiff of PR can often send readers clicking elsewhere.

As you blog, you should also contact other notable blogs within your industry to see if they would be interested in posting about your work. When contacting other blogs, be sure to get in touch with the ones whose style best fits your own and whose audience is most likely to respond to your type of work. And, just like traditional press, write a personal e-mail to one blog editor at a time (from your top pick down), and contact another blog only if you don't hear back from your first choice after a couple weeks. Bloggers do not want to find themselves posting about the same thing as someone else.

Matt Armendariz is driven. Starting as a grocery bagger for Whole Foods Market, he rose through the ranks and emerged five years later as an art director for the company's San Francisco office. All this without any design training. So it isn't surprising that Matt would then leave the company to start a new career in photography (again, an area where he had no formal training) with nothing but an obsession for food and a blog. After eighteen years in the food business and five years as the blogger behind Mattbites, he's worked for clients such as POM Wonderful, FIJI Water, Bristol Farms, and *Time* magazine. Incredibly, he was even invited to appear on the *Martha Stewart Show* to teach Martha how to make his favorite cookie recipe during an episode she devoted to blogging. Matt shows us that, even when you succeed in one thing, sometimes you have to challenge yourself and find new motivation. For him, photography was the new summit to climb. With training that was equal parts on-the-job and self-taught, Matt is a clear example of how far you really can go with an unstoppable go-getter attitude.

How did you develop your design and photography skills on your own?
As a child I was always taking newspaper circulars and reassembling them in different formats or creating magazine covers from drawings and photocopying my creations for my parents. Let's just say I had an active imagination! I didn't realize what I was doing was graphic design until much later in life. And after a trip to Universal Studios in the mid-'70s I became obsessed with the ideas of sets and facades for movies and photography. I began to build things in the garage and change my room to reflect a certain location. In my early twenties I took a job with Whole Foods Market bagging groceries. One day I hopped on an old Mac computer and used PageMaker to make some sale signs for a few departments. I quickly realized that the desktop publishing tools were exactly what I was looking for! I became their store artist. Some of my work got noticed by the Chicago Academy of Sciences, which started a really amazing freelance relationship with me. I started designing many of their collateral pieces. I became obsessed with graphic design and spent not only my work hours doing it but also every

bit of free time. My job at Whole Foods allowed me to get my feet wet not only with graphic design but production and printing as well. That really helped me to develop skills in lieu of schooling, which also led to my growth creatively within the Whole Foods brand.

As for my photography skills, I'm completely self-taught as well. Now I should back up and say that, because I art directed so many food photo shoots, I felt as if I had the best classroom to learn in. I did a lot of reading to understand the technical aspects of photography like shutter speed and f-stops. But I mainly learned from practicing. My partner likes to joke that I literally never set down my camera for two entire years.

What made you decide to switch to photography and to freelancing?

I was art directing tons of food photo shoots for Whole Foods, and I wanted to see if I could produce a project from beginning to end. I picked up a camera, began shooting, and realized how amazing it felt to have an idea, direct it, shoot it, and design it. It was a very powerful concept for me, and it stuck. I made the switch to photography for several reasons. I discovered that I could make more money than I ever could through design. But I only share this as a fact; I'm not motivated by greed, believe me! It's an entirely different ball game with much higher stakes. It's no better or harder or easier than graphic design; it's just a different market. But I liked the fact that I was creating something that encompassed my entire creative being: color, product or subject knowledge, perspective, balance, composition, humor, energy, all of it.

What are your favorite types of jobs to work on?

I can't really say I have a favorite type of job. It depends on my mood or whim. Each type of job has its advantages and disadvantages. Sometimes shooting photos of people is so much fun, as the interaction is crucial. And then sometimes I love being alone with food on a very small set with just a few people. On one hand, editorial work can be much more liberating, but on the other hand, I do enjoy the exacting nature of advertising at times. It's like trying to solve a big puzzle. I may not have a favorite job, but I do have a favorite style of working. For the most part, I don't really mind what I'm shooting as long as I like the team and the client—that's the most important thing.

What made you decide to start your blog, Mattbites?

Because I was in the food business already and dealing with the creation of visuals, there were interesting things and extra details that I didn't have space for in my work, whether stories, anecdotes, outtakes from a photo shoot, or a peek into the lives of the people I've met. I started my blog as a way to share those extra tidbits, and it became a liberating place where I could say anything about food without being limited by a project or a client. Having a blog creates an automatic means of networking, as I can stay in touch with other food bloggers and photographers who blog. And sometimes a bunch of us food bloggers in L.A. will get together in person for dinners or to host events. I love the people I've met through my blog.

How has the popularity of your blog helped you to gain more exposure and new work?

My first freelance photo client was Border Grill, a restaurant in Los Angeles who approached me through my blog. I hadn't even switched over to doing photography full-time. I've never had to go out and find work. All my jobs have been through referrals and from my blog or Web site. But my blog has been the number one thing in helping me get work. I'm very lucky that all my years in the food business afforded me tons of contacts and that blogging has increased my visibility. In my blog, I'm able to show not only an image but also describe the process behind it. When I was art directing and hiring photographers, it was very important to me that I enjoyed whom I was working with. I think through my blog, potential clients can see a bit of me and can decide if they want to work with me. It's the best calling card.

With so many blogs out there now, do you have any suggestions for newbies looking to use their own blog as a promotion tool?

If you're going to start a blog in hopes that it will also promote your business, make sure that whatever you do, you have high-quality content, whether writing or photos, to share with readers. You have to offer something different. If you're not willing to work at blogging and put in the time, it's going to be difficult. Know that you won't make a million dollars off your blog, and it should always serve as an adjunct to something else.

Advertising

Word of mouth may prove to be your best advertiser, but traditional advertising can be a great way to get the buzz going. Industry magazines, publications, and Web sites sometimes offer advertising space in a variety of sizes and prices. There are also talent resource directories (e.g., *The Black Book*) that advertising agencies and design firms keep on hand to quickly find freelance illustrators, photographers, and more. These annual publications usually include a full-page sample of each listed freelancer's work, along with contact numbers. Finally, check blogs that your potential clients may read and consider buying an advertising spot there. It's usually a pretty quick and inexpensive way to get more exposure fast.

Getting a Leg Up on the Competition

Within all creative fields, you'll find competitions. You can enter a film festival with a short film you've produced. You can submit your recycled-industrial felt chair to a sustainable furniture design competition. The logo and letterhead you designed for a new restaurant can be considered for a graphic design annual. Browse through trade magazines and specialty Web sites to see who holds competitions and take note of the times of the year in which the entries are due. Book publishers also highlight creative work with books focused on such topics as the year's best packaging design, fashion illustrations, handwritten typography, and more. Browse through a bookstore and note the names of publishers who regularly produce these types of books. Entering competitions will put your work in front of boldface industry names who jury and judge them. And winning awards and competitions means you can attach the label "award-winning" to your work—not to mention get the satisfaction of peer and industry approval. It also makes good fodder for your regular newsletter or blog. As with marketing, anything new and exciting is an opportunity to talk about your work and expose it to more people.

Networking and Referrals

As any veteran freelancer will tell you, the relationships you forge are instrumental to being successful. Many business opportunities are built on word of mouth or serendipitous encounters with people in your business and personal spheres. Though you could get a lot of work through word of mouth, it doesn't mean you should wait around for opportunity to strike. Seek out events attended by your potential clientele or gatherings with other freelancers in your field. But don't stop there—networking requires followthrough. Look into every lead you find and connection you make. But even if every human contact you have, or will have, carries the potential of a future professional relationship, that doesn't mean you should approach every person with a salesperson mentality. Self-promotion and networking aren't about merely placing a card in someone's hand or wearing your business on your sleeve—it's about building genuine relationships.

Word-of-mouth referrals can come from all types of sources, but most likely they will come from those who have already worked with you successfully or who just really like you and want to see you succeed (Mom and Dad included). Also, if you know other creatives who do the same type of work, they may refer you to their clients when they are too busy to handle the job or if they feel you may be a better fit. Regardless of where the referral comes from, make sure to thank the person who has so kindly passed on your name.

If you had a good relationship with a previous employer, chances are they could use your talents until your replacement has been hired or if they have projects in need of your skills. Rather than finding a brandnew freelancer who isn't familiar with their work, it's likely they'd prefer to outsource the work to a past employee who knows the protocol. Get in touch with your old boss and announce your freelance status. Chances are she'll enjoy hearing from you, and your name will be put at the top of the list when they hire freelance talent or are asked for a referral.

Virtual Networking

The good thing about this business is that clients can essentially be anywhere—and you can find them in places you'd least expect. Because any connection could be a potential lead, don't be afraid to connect with those you meet through blogs or online forums. Or you can use social networking sites like Facebook, LinkedIn, and Twitter to connect with individuals you know. But keep in mind that using social networking avenues can be risky—be careful not to divulge too much information about yourself. Remember that every posting or word you say is an open invitation into your life, and it may affect how potential clients view you as a professional. You can juggle both personal and business networking by starting a professional page on one of these sites in addition to your personal page. Clients don't need to hear about that rager you went to last night, and your friends may not be interested in hearing about every update on your business. Keeping things focused on business, and keeping the personal talk to a minimum, will increase the likelihood that you'll find both potential clients and a network of creative freelancers along the way.

Mailings

You'd be surprised at how many companies are interested in hiring freelance talent but don't because they don't have the time or bandwidth to review hundreds of new résumés. This is the case where outreach mixed with a go-getter approach can make you the standout option. These days, "cold calling" doesn't necessarily have to involve an actual phone call. It's much more effective to send a simple and well-written letter or e-mail to tell potential clients that you like their work, to outline how your style complements theirs, and to tell the clients that you would love to work with them. It also helps to attach a few samples of your work that best fits their brands, so they can quickly and easily see what you do. You won't hear back from everyone, but chances are you'll get a response from some of them. Even if they don't need your skills right away, they'll keep you in mind for the future if you (or your work) piqued their interest.

If someone likes an item you've designed enough to keep it out on her desk, it's likely she will remember you for a future project.

You also can send small promotional mailings such as postcards or e-mail newsletters. While a single mailing may not score you a gig immediately, strong, repetitive mailings could eventually land you plum jobs. Also consider sending other types of promotional pieces, such as a custom-made calendar or notepad that will serve as a daily reminder of you and your work. If someone likes an item you've designed enough to keep it out on her desk, it's likely she will remember you for a future project. Whatever you choose to send, remember that it must grab the viewer's attention immediately. Be clever with text and visuals, without being obnoxious. The more creative you are with mailings, the more likely you are to get responses.

Who will get these mailings? You'll need to create a database of people and companies. Create a contact list that includes both people you know and those you want to know. To compile a strong list, whenever you meet a contact, make it a practice to write down his information. Make a list of everyone you know and look in magazines for companies that might be interested in your work. If you have a specific goal or philosophy, look for companies you think would be compatible with it. Do your best to keep your list up to date with the name of the current human resources manager, art director, or other relevant contact at each company.

Follow-up is key in marketing programs—there's no point in sending out promotional pieces if you are never going to follow up on leads. But the trick is following up without coming off as pushy or a nuisance. So after you send out a few mailings, you should reconnect with an e-mail within a couple weeks—but send no more than two follow-up e-mails. In addition to all this virtual communication, if you get a positive response, ask if you can come in to show your portfolio in person or have an informational interview. By definition, something virtual doesn't quite compare to the real thing; you can better establish a relationship with a potential client in person. You may be invited to attend a meeting or to pitch for a project.

MARKETING WRITING

Your marketing materials can't be all visual and zero verbal. Together with good visuals, writing makes your work come alive and communicates your story. Your goal should be get your message across using as little jargon as possible. Be brief without sacrificing ideas or style and aim to elicit a positive response. To achieve this, you need to be clear and graceful in your word choices. If you're not the most confident writer, find a consultant who can help write project description copy, a sensible business letter, or a bio for your Web site. If you're tight on cash, here's an opportunity to barter with a copywriter. Before finalizing anything (and especially if you didn't have copywriter help), ask a friend or colleague to proofread your prose. Oftentimes others will pick up on spelling errors or a lack of cohesiveness that you didn't notice, and they might offer helpful suggestions for making it stronger.

Ongoing Marketing Plans

Every day, clients are faced with a sea of choices. Ultimately, it is the unusual that will snag their attention. As more and more creatives pursue solitary careers, standing out from the crowd isn't always easy. But just because the playing field is getting more crowded, that doesn't mean there isn't room for something new. Just look at social-networking sites: first Friendster ruled; then MySpace was cued for world domination; and later Facebook became the new black. Surely, another start-up will take the lead. Likewise, you will have predecessors and competitors—but the thing is, they aren't you. When you offer something different, a funny thing happens—the playing field shifts, and new pathways open up. So you'll need to use some marketing tactics to ensure that you stand out. Keep your Web site updated with new work. Enter competitions and try to win awards. Write a blog and get blogged about. These are but a few ways to ensure visibility. Stay fresh in everyone's mind, and you'll get your name to regularly punctuate conversations among clients and peers in your industry.

Look at yourself from an outsider's perspective, and through this challenge you'll learn about your market's needs and how to articulately present your own work.

Of course, tooting your own horn doesn't come easily to everyone. If the thought of marketing yourself makes you cringe or conjures ideas of overtly sales-driven advertising campaigns, try this exercise: Be your own client. Look at yourself from an outsider's perspective, and through this challenge you'll learn about your market's needs and how to articulately present your own work.

A sound self-promotion strategy needs to focus on the following goals:

01 Acquiring new clients. Your goal is to get your work in front of new clients and focus on arranging to show your portfolio in person.

02 Client retention. Keep in contact with people you've worked with or who have expressed interest in your work. The main tool for this is database maintenance and developing regular mailings.

03 Profile building. Raise your profile through recognition and endorsements. Here, the strategy will be primarily PR-based: getting media interviews, getting mentions in articles and books, giving speeches, and speaking on industry panels.

The ultimate goal of marketing is to get a steady stream of clients and projects requiring your particular vision.

As you formulate your marketing plans, remember that they don't need to be elaborate, but it helps to write everything down. Goals and objectives tend to become more real and less daunting when you can see them in writing. Keeping a record will help you clarify your ideas so that you can see your plans mature and change over time. When marketing plans are executed well, they can shape the direction of your business and allow you to take jobs you really want instead of accepting jobs just to keep your business afloat. Even if you have more than enough work coming in, it's important to continue marketing and prospecting to guarantee work for the years to come.

The ultimate goal of marketing is to get a steady stream of clients and projects requiring your particular vision. With time, you may find that getting your target audience's attention is child's play compared to keeping it. You need to maintain the attention on you beyond the first moment your work fascinates your clients. When you're just starting out, your strategies and budget will most likely be modest, but your marketing efforts can still yield impressive results—especially if you exploit every avenue available and act with a sense of energy and consistency.

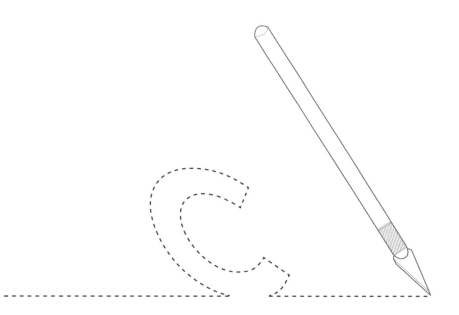

CHAPTER

4

 WORKING WITH CLIENTS

Like any successful friendship or marriage, clients require love, dedication, and trust to foster a long-term, happy relationship. When you're new to freelancing, this dynamic can be challenging. You'll have to develop customer service and communication skills to clearly express your creative vision and achieve client satisfaction. In this chapter, we'll give you the lowdown on all things client related, including the types of clients you could be working with and how to communicate with buyers, as well as how to attract the right customers. The more you understand your clients, the more likely you are to guarantee their happiness with a project. This is incredibly beneficial for your freelance future: happy clients will be more likely to pay you on time, hire you again for future gigs, and possibly refer you to others for jobs.

Client 101

San Francisco Chronicle. Bank of America. A local design firm. Your dentist. Any number of businesses may be in need of your freelance talents. They run the gamut from small to large, independent to corporate. At large companies, you'll often work with a creative director, art director, or editor who will assign and oversee your work. For small or start-up companies, the founder may be your sole contact. Whether you're looking to be the go-to for small, local companies or you're reaching skyward for the big corporations, here's a closer look at the types of clients who may require your services:

Print editorial

This category includes magazines, newspapers, and other periodicals. Editorial buyers hire freelancers regularly to style props, photograph images, create illustrations, or design layouts for articles or magazine covers.

Entertainment industry

You really can't throw a brick in the entertainment industry without hitting a freelancer. Television and film production companies are staffed practically wall-to-wall with freelance talent. They recruit freelancers across a broad range of fields, from motion graphics for their movie titles and illustrators for posters and sales presentations to producers and stylists for shoots. Because entertainment gigs are project based, freelancers in this sector will be hired for blocks of time while projects are in progress.

Book publishing

Book publishers turn to freelancers for photographs, styling, illustrations, or designs needed to grace a book cover or depict a story. They may also hire you to create marketing materials to promote these books.

Ad agencies and design firms

Agencies and firms are usually staffed by a variety of creative types, but they do outsource work to freelancers when they need a particular style or skill set that they lack in-house. In this case, the agency is your client, even though they are hiring you to help create work for one of their clients.

Small private companies

Small businesses and start-up companies often turn to freelancers for their creative needs because they often prefer to work with other small, independent businesses. A nice perk in this relationship is that you'll likely have the opportunity to work directly with the heads of the companies.

Large public companies

Whether they're in the Fortune 500 or are just a large public company, bigger companies often work with their human resources department or intermediaries such as agents or advertising agencies to find freelance talent. Without an agent, freelancers can find it challenging to get on the inside track with large companies, since it's often hard to find out exactly who the contact person is.

Commissions

Often a one-time project, a commission is typically an original piece of your work that is created for a person or institution and is considered public artwork. For example, you could be asked to illustrate a mural for a children's hospital, create a film to honor a museum's founder for its annual gala, or shoot a still-life photo for the lobby of a luxury hotel.

Personal

If your work is out in public (i.e., on your Web site or promoted on a blog), a regular Joe may fall in love with your aesthetic and ask you to design his wedding invitations, photograph her new baby, or create a watercolor portrait of his beloved pooch.

Getting their art commissioned by the *New York Times*, especially for a magazine or section cover, is the Holy Grail for many freelance artists. Aviva Michaelov, the art director for the *New York Times*'s Op-Ed (opposite the editorial page) section, candidly discusses with us the process by which she, along with the editors, selected artists to visually communicate the most important stories of the week during her former position as art director of Week in Review. With newspapers, an artist's ability to quickly turn assignments around is crucial. But the Week in Review section is even more immediate and demanding; commissions often have to be completed within one to three days. If you are an illustrator who can swiftly and efficiently take conceptual ideas and create strongly narrative artwork, you may very well have a calling at the *New York Times*. Certainly, an endorsement from this prestigious publication would be an impressive feather in your cap.

How do you choose a freelance illustrator to work with?

Usually I envision how a cover or story should look, and then I pick an illustrator whose style would best fit the concept. A good portion of the Week in Review stories are conceptual and require smart solutions, so I always look for illustrators who are good problem solvers and can come up with a strong concept that they can also execute.

When searching for a freelance illustrator, I often turn to *American Illustration* books, refer to my RSS feeds from several sites that link to new visual sites and projects, or check the notes, names, and Web sites that I've accumulated over time. Whenever I come across an interesting illustration or drawing in a magazine, gallery, or bookstore, I'll look up the artist's Web site to see their full body of work. So there's a lot of online browsing and navigating that I do to find new and exciting artists.

Is a freelancer's level of experience ever a consideration in your selection process?

There are several illustrators I work with on a regular basis because I know they can turn around the work I need, but I do try to use a new illustrator every week if I can. I will experiment with beginners for spot illustrations, but I often stick with pros for the cover, since that image carries a lot of weight. More experienced, older illustrators are also more likely to follow the news and know the topics I call them about (the economy, politics, history), which makes the process easier when we're conceptualizing the illustration together.

How crucial is a freelancer's efficiency and ability to quickly complete a project?

Because the Week in Review is a weekly section, my freelancers have between one and three days to conceptualize, draw sketches, and complete the final piece. Sometimes it even happens all in one day! And, yes, the time constraints do affect my choice of illustrators. There are so many wonderful illustrators out there who I, unfortunately, cannot use for Week in Review, because their style requires more time to execute the job. As a result, the style of illustrations we use tend to be bold, simple, and direct.

Do you have standard fees you pay artists? Is the fee negotiable?

There are standard fees for the Week in Review section. Unfortunately, for most assignments, it means there isn't much room for negotiation, as the budget only allows me to pay everyone the same flat rate, regardless of their level of experience. Occasionally, when I have more complicated assignments and a different budget, there can be room for rate negotiations.

Can you tell us about the process of working with a freelancer?

After our weekly story meeting, I discuss with my editor and photo editor how to best visualize the stories, by photo or illustration. Since Week in Review is tied to developing, ongoing stories, our plan changes regularly, based on how the news develops over the week. Once we decide on a general concept and style needed, I would choose an illustrator, for instance, and call to confirm that he or she is available. In my discussions with him or her, I would describe the story, the schedule, and the budget. And often, I would need sketches the very next day! I might discuss this over the phone or by e-mail, but regardless, the illustrator would always receive an e-mail with the job brief attached.

After receiving the sketches, I would discuss with the artist which idea he or she prefers and why. I enjoy hearing their process and the reasoning why one concept is stronger than another. If I foresee anything that could be strengthened, I might have the illustrator make revisions before presenting the sketches. Once I've narrowed down my favorite sketches, I would present one or more to my editor to discuss which one works best. If the sketch is approved, I would notify the illustrator and provide him or her with the final specs to work from. If for any reason my editor doesn't approve the sketch, then we would go into a second round of sketches. Before sending the final high-resolution file, illustrators usually send me a preview to approve. And then, once printed, the illustrator's credit goes along with the illustration on both the print and Web versions. Believe it or not, this whole process usually happens within a matter of two days!

Do you have any advice for a freelancer who wants to get hired by the *New York Times*?

The best way to submit work to us is to research the sections you'd like to work for and get contact information for those editors from our administrator. E-mail us the links to your Web site or portfolio or send a letter in the mail with samples of your work. While most freelancers are those I have found, some have been those who have contacted me directly and initiated interest. I also work with illustrators from all over the world. Especially when a story is about a specific location, I try to find an illustrator from that region who has a little more background information and may be better at conceptualizing the piece.

Getting the Job

Consider this situation: The phone rings or an e-mail appears in your in-box from a potential client inquiring about your creative services. What is your first inclination? It may feel natural to break out the bubbly while imagining the amazing four-page illustration spreads you'll produce, but it's important to pause before leaping into action. You need to make sure the job is the right fit for you and convince the client that you're the one to pick. Arrange a meeting to discuss the job more specifically and solidify the prospective project's details. Whether you are meeting in person or via a conference call, the steps from a client inquiry to landing the job are the same. We'll go into more detail on the monetary and contractual aspects in the next chapter, but here are the components for discussing (and hopefully landing) a new client job:

Presenting your work or portfolio

Before meeting with a potential client, make sure you have a good understanding of what they do, what the project is, and what style of work they are looking for. Then customize your portfolio to entice them. Rather than show everything in your arsenal, highlight eight to twelve examples of your work that are most relevant to their needs. For example, if a prospective client needs an illustration to go on hangtags for her clothing company and is interested in a quirky and whimsical style, show her samples of your most fanciful work, as well as illustrations you've created for other fashion brands. Depending on the meeting format, you can present your work in the form of a printed portfolio, an electronic PDF, or highlighted works on your Web site. You should choose a presentation format that will best display your work within the context of your meeting. Also, tell the client about your past experience, if any, and how your work will benefit her company. Approach everything with a positive attitude—never sell yourself short, don't draw attention to things you don't know how to do, and don't apologize for any weakness in your work. Finally, make sure you have a business card, résumé, or leave-behind with your contact information.

Getting the information and understanding the job

The client will most likely provide an overall description of the project, their responsibilities and needs, and where you fit in. Research as much as you can about your potential client. If you can't find the answers to these questions beforehand, here are a few good questions to ask your client: What's your service, style, and overall aesthetic? Who are your target clients or customers? What distinguishes you from your competitors? Who are some of your current or future competitors? What's your end goal for this project? Get as many specifics as you can when you meet the client, so you can put together an accurate job brief and proposal that covers everything you've discussed.

Timing and deadlines

Even in early discussions, it's important to know the job schedule and project deadlines so that you can assess if you can realistically complete the job within the specified timeframe. Timing may rule you out from the beginning if your schedule is already booked up or you plan to be out of town during a period that the client considers crucial for the assignment. Also, if the deadline is tight, you can gauge how much, if any, extra rush fees you'll need to charge to complete the job on time. You should also give the client an estimate of when he should expect to hear from you with a proposal.

Creating a job brief

Using the information you've gathered from the introductory meeting, organize your notes and thoughts into a job brief that outlines the particulars of the project. The components of a job brief include a description of the client, the client's problem or need, the competition, the audience, the message or purpose of the job, the means of accomplishing it (your creative service), and an estimated schedule of due dates. You can type this out as a simple Word document and print it on your letterhead. If you're missing any information to complete the brief, be sure to follow up with the client to collect the pertinent information.

Job proposal

A job proposal is the combination of a job brief and an estimate. The estimate factors in your hourly rate, the project time line, the value of the work, and, most important, the total cost for the job. If you know the client's expected budget, you will have a better opportunity to put together a realistic estimate. Based on your proposal, the client will either choose to hire you, negotiate the cost, or go elsewhere. (See Estimates, page 104.)

Accepting the job and signing a contract

Once a client has accepted your proposal, she may present you with a contract to solidify the terms agreed upon. If she doesn't, you should put together a contract for both parties to sign. We'll discuss how to put together your own contract in the next chapter. Never start a project without a signed contract.

Turning down a job

Should you decide a project isn't right for you, you should tell the client as soon as possible. It's okay to tell him that you can't work within his budget, that your schedule is too booked to meet the deadline, or that you feel you're not the right match for the project. If you simply don't want to work on the project, you may not feel comfortable giving that as your reason. Instead, you can offer a polite response that you're just unavailable to work on the project. And, if you can, refer the client to other freelancers who may be more suitable for the job. He'll appreciate your honesty and your help in suggesting someone else to work with.

Interpreting rejection

You won't land every job prospect that comes your way. Often, you simply won't hear back from a client, and that will be your sign that she went elsewhere. Whether it's due to cost, your level of experience, or a clash in personalities, a rejection isn't the end of the world. Remember that even when you don't land projects, the opportunity to present your work is a learning experience that will help you improve your future dealings with potential clients. Don't spend too much time looking back; take the lessons you've learned and apply them to whatever comes next.

Weeding out Bad Clients

The best clients not only will offer a project that excites you but also will believe in your abilities, trust your instincts, and welcome your constructive feedback. They will be great communicators, and they will come to you with the hope that this is just the beginning of a long-term relationship. How can you discern a dream client from a problematic one? Before an initial meeting, try to learn as much as you can about a prospective client. On the off chance that the client has a bad reputation among freelancers, you may find negative banter in an online forum, or the client may have been given a low rating by the Better Business Bureau. Ask as many questions as possible about a potential job to acquaint yourself with the client and the project to ensure it's a good fit. The more you know, the better equipped you'll be to weed out those clients you may later regret taking on.

Oftentimes, troublesome personality traits or poor communication skills that you pick up on in initial conversations are telltale signs of how the client will behave when you actually work with him.

Regardless of the job, learn to trust your instincts when meeting a potential buyer. Does he seem flaky or unfocused? Does she have a brash or condescending attitude? Is he already trying to nickel-and-dime your services while insisting your fees are overpriced? Is she slow to respond to messages? Oftentimes, troublesome personality traits or poor communication skills that you pick up on in initial conversations are telltale signs of how the client will behave when you actually work with him. A nickel-and-dimer may question every hour billed on a project; an unfocused buyer may request a never-ending list of changes; a slow communicator may draw out a project for longer than you anticipated. Any issues you notice in initial meetings will likely play out on a larger scale when the client hires you for the job.

However, when you're green to the freelancing business, you may not have the option of being selective about your clients. With potentially sticky projects, you'll probably have to consider whether the caliber of the project outweighs the problems that may come up. In the paying-your-dues stage, it may simply be more important to accrue projects for your portfolio. But, as you get busier and more sought after, you'll reach that point where you're able to pick and choose whom to work with, and you'll learn more about finding clients who are complementary to your business practices.

Approaching the Project

Like an actor preparing for a new role, do your homework and immerse yourself in areas of a particular project that you are not familiar with. Read up on your client's industry as well as their business standing within it. Are they established pioneers or relatively unknown? What trends exist within their field? Who are their competitors? By understanding the full scope of where they are positioned within the market, you can better conceptualize creative material that is right for them and will help them stand out from the competition. Next, research the specific topic of the project. If you're creating a Web site for an ice-cream shop with an old-fashioned parlor atmosphere, engage yourself in the specifics of everything related to ice cream, dessert, and retro restaurants. For instance, check out other ice-cream shops and visit your local flea market for old parlor photos, vintage store signs, and typographic inspiration.

FIRST CLIENTS

When you're starting out, it can be tempting to go after clients who have a history of projects with a great design sensibility. But if they are well-known among creatives, it is likely they already have a stable of freelancers they work with. It's not a complete waste of time to chase big-name clients, but at the early stages of your freelance career, it's probably best to invest your resources going after smaller companies or organizations that will more eagerly appreciate your talents. Seek out clients who you think would give you the opportunity to do groundbreaking work for them. They could even be nonprofit organizations with small budgets. Though they may not be able to compensate you as well as larger companies could, the work you do for them could certainly pad your portfolio with great projects.

Maintaining Communication

With the global reach of the Internet, you can score a client in Paris, Texas, or Paris, France. You can shoot a quick e-mail from your chaise longue on the beach as easily as you can from your desk chair in the studio. It's common for freelancers to build a client base that includes both local and long-distance clients. But being in the same time zone as your client and available at short notice will often be in your favor. Clients usually appreciate a freelancer whom they can easily meet face to face and who is available for last-minute meetings or unexpected issues. But it's also common these days to work with long-distance clients if a potential buyer likes what he sees in your online portfolio and hasn't found similar talent locally. Remote clients require communication via phone, e-mail, or video chat in place of in-person powwows. Your communication tactics must be especially strong when dealing with long-distance clients, because you won't have the advantage of in-person meetings to sell your concepts and ideas. You'll have to be able to clearly verbalize over the phone or write well-constructed explanations to accompany your visuals.

Regardless of where your client is located, clear and constructive communication from the very beginning of a project will likely lead to a successful end result. Start every project with a detailed timeline that incorporates the client's final deadline, your schedule, and the benchmark deadlines along the way. Between deadlines, keep buyers abreast of your progress with a quick call or e-mail; they'll feel reassured to know their job is your priority.

At the beginning of every job, ask what type of communication your client prefers. If they're local, do they prefer in-person presentations, or will they be comfortable monitoring your progress through e-mail and phone updates? If they're long distance, are they comfortable giving feedback via e-mail, or would they rather talk over the phone or via video chat? Would they prefer to receive e-mailed PDFs and then discuss on the phone, or would they rather have you come in to their office and give a presentation to the entire department?

After seeing your work, a client review can go one of three ways: they love it, they hate it, or they like it and have some recommended changes. In most cases, your first idea won't be the final product, so when you are receiving client feedback it's important to listen to the criticism and make sure you understand exactly why they don't like something. Sometimes, concepts you think are clear winners are not even close to the client's desires. Let's say you've presented six designs for initial logo concepts for a line of gourmet cheeses. The client likes options one, four, and six but cannot describe exactly why. Ask what she is responding to—does she like the typefaces, icons, colors, or layout? Sometimes clients cannot separate pieces of the various options they like. If possible, dissect the visuals so you can see if there are aspects from the different concepts that can be combined into a new hybrid concept. Maybe it's as simple as covering up some parts of the design to look at each element separately. Ask questions like, "Are there any specific parts of the logos that you don't like, and why?" "What parts are you most drawn to, and why?" Questions like these can help you eliminate elements clients are unhappy with and proceed with the characteristics they like.

Be objective and remove your emotions so that you can offer suggestions with a clear head and their best interests in mind.

When reviewing your work with clients, take the time to explain your ideas in detail, so they have a clear understanding of how the concept will change or grow as it reaches the final stages of execution. Also, make sure they know what answers or decisions you need from them in order to proceed to the next phase of revisions. From the ideas you've presented, clients may ask for your input on what you feel is the best option. Some clients don't work with freelancers often, so it's okay to guide them through the process. As a general rule, don't let criticism become personal. Be objective and remove your emotions so that you can offer suggestions with a clear head and their best interests in mind. If you respond well to client feedback and quickly offer thoughts on how you'll approach the next round, you'll be on your way to an end product you'll both be proud of.

GIVING CLIENTS PROJECT OPTIONS

Before presenting work to a client, decide up front how many options you'll present. The number of options will vary depending on whether you're working on an animated clip, a logo, or a set of props for a photo shoot. More than one option is always best, so the client can compare and more effectively respond to what he likes or doesn't like. Clients can't always imagine things they can't see, so giving them more to respond to is ideal. With every round, you should be presenting fewer options as you whittle down to the final pick. As you gain more experience, you'll figure out how many creative options tend to work best, as well as that magic number that gives a client enough options for comparison.

Unhappy Clients and Canceled Jobs

Something's different: you're put off by something a client said (or didn't say) in response to your work. Maybe she's having a hard time giving you feedback or direction, and the project seems to have stalled. Maybe she used to get excited about your work, and now her interest feels lackluster. These changes may cause you to suspect that your client isn't totally happy with your work. Rather than wait to hear specifics from the client, check in before the problem gets worse. You may be able to nip the problem in the bud by showing your extra attention, desire to make her happy, and commitment to giving her the product she was hoping for.

Despite your best efforts, however, sometimes a client will simply be unhappy with your work and will choose to stop the project short. Clients may not want to tell you they've hired someone else who was a better fit, so if you aren't sure why they have chosen to cancel a job, simply ask. It will help you in the long run to know how the project could have worked out better and what you can do next time to avoid repeating the offense. (See Cancellation policy and kill fees, page 106.) Regardless of the reasoning behind the canceled job, you must persevere; everyone encounters rejection at some point. Learn from your mistakes and stay positive about the possibilities ahead.

Boomerang Buyers

Clients respond well to a freelancer's passion for a project, enthusiasm for new ideas, and great communication throughout the process. So, once you've completed a successful project and your newfound client has learned to trust you, this relationship is likely to result in more work. Sometimes a new assignment will come immediately, but oftentimes you won't be exactly sure if or when they'll be back in touch. If it's been several months since a buyer has hired you for a project, be proactive. Initiate a simple e-mail or phone call to ask how things are going and if there are any upcoming projects you can help them with. It's also a great idea to keep clients up to date on your work by sending out a monthly or quarterly e-newsletter or postcard announcing recent awards, press coverage, or new work you've completed. Seeing your growth and success validates their choice in hiring you, reminds them you're out there, and shows you're valued by other companies as well. Also, simple gestures like sending out a holiday card or small gift at the end of the year will let clients know you appreciate their business. It will serve your business well if you consistently retain a handful of return clients. Boomerang buyers add stability to your income and regularity of work, which are the backbone of any freelance career.

For Amy Ruppel, inspiration and luck seem to strike when she least expects it. During the collage portion of an encaustic-painting class in 2004, she made a simple decision to incorporate printouts of her computer-illustrated bird silhouettes and striped patterns. The result was the perfect marriage of digital and handmade, a painting that brought together the best of both of her artistic talents. At the time, Amy was holding down a steady job designing ads for the yellow pages, and the class was just a way to explore her creativity. Little did she know that her encaustic paintings were about to be the next "it" thing on the Web. She started innocently enough, putting her paintings for sale on her self-designed Web site and notifying her mailing list of mostly friends. Soon thereafter, two big breaks came in the form of a DailyCandy e-mail newsletter and a blog mention on Design*Sponge. Suddenly, Amy's work was in high demand, from art shows to freelance commissions to licensing deals. Although Amy estimates that freelance work accounts for only 25 percent of her business, she's acquired some prominent clients, such as Target and Converse. So, fine artists take note: freelancing commercially can open up a viable source of income, not to mention a rewarding creative outlet.

Do you have any formal training in illustration or design?

I attended the University of Wisconsin in Milwaukee and received a degree in fine arts and creative writing. I didn't study anything in terms of design or illustration. My boyfriend at the time was a graphic designer, and he taught me Illustrator and Photoshop after I graduated. With those skills, I was able to land some design jobs. As for illustration, I've been drawing all my life, and I get a lot of inspiration from children's books. I attended an illustrators' conference in 2000, where I met my illustration heroes, like Anita Kunz and Brad Holland, and it really inspired me to get into it.

How did you start working with Target? What was that process like?

They just called me up out of the blue and asked if I would be interested in being the designer for Holiday 2007. It was great endorsement, because they had asked designer Tord Boontje in Holiday 2006. Later, I found out that one of the in-house designers at Target had one of my wax paintings in her cubicle, and that's where they got the idea to ask me. It was very serendipitous. When I agreed to the project, they asked me how many people worked at my studio. The funny thing is, I work alone. They told me that I would need a production crew and set me up with BBDO, an advertising agency in New York. So basically, I created the illustrations and handed them off to BBDO and Target. BBDO turned them into in-store decorations and end caps [a coveted piece of real estate in a store's layout located at the end of each aisle in a high traffic area]. And Target used them as surface designs on some holiday products, like boxed chocolates, window clings, candle tins, and gift bags. I also created the backgrounds for five Target holiday commercials. It was a seven-month process to complete all the work. The Target job has been the biggest project I've gotten, and the most fun as well.

What effect did the Target job have on your career?

Strangely, the Target job had an opposite effect on my freelance work. It actually hurt me. Before I landed the Target job, people were calling me constantly to design them a logo or a draw an illustration. Then suddenly, all the calls stopped. I'm not sure why, but perhaps some of these smaller companies assumed they couldn't afford me anymore. Before the Target deal, I never really had to go out and find work.

What types of companies are licensing your illustrations?

I have my illustrations on magnets and paperweights at iPop, an alphabet series for Blik Graphics, Burton snowboards, stationery for Vigo cards, and lunch boxes for Aladdin, to name a few. All of these companies approached me. However, these days I am contacting companies on my own. I look for companies who seem really fun and places where my illustrations would fit in.

Are big-name clients overly controlling?

I've been lucky to work with Converse and Target as both have been a great collaborative process. They are open to suggestions and respectful of my work. And, likewise, I have to remember to be open to change and new ideas, because I'm working with good designers and art directors who may know something or see something that I don't. The thing about big companies is that anything you submit has to go through so many channels. They are also so busy that communication can be slow sometimes. But other than that, there aren't any major drawbacks.

Have you considered working with an agent?

I've been thinking of getting an agent these days to get more work. For me, the only downside of having an agent is that I'll be talking through a person, which means I may not always get the pleasure of working with a client directly. For me, it's nice to speak with the client directly, to get a feel for that person and the full sense of what they want.

As a fine artist, what do you find interesting about freelance illustration?

It's given me the ability to show my range. Oftentimes, I'm commissioned to do illustrations that don't resemble my paintings, and I enjoy that. For example, in my work for Converse, I've illustrated kittens and puppies. Though my birds are popular, they can't last forever, so it's nice to have a portfolio of illustration work showing a variety of things I've done. Plus, it's nice not to be inundated with the same types of commission requests.

Licensing Your Work

There are dreams, and then there are the realities of being a freelancer: work can dry up at any point. So it's up to you to be a proactive agent for your work, finding as many income opportunities as possible. In additional to doing project-based work, you can find clients who will license your artwork or designs to be used on a variety of products, from melamine plates and notebooks to backpacks and fabric. Or if you are a photographer or filmmaker, you can sell your photography or film clips to stock photography agencies or film bureaus. The best part of licensing is that you can earn income from artwork you've already created. Whether you are paid a flat fee or receive royalties (a monthly or quarterly check reflecting your commission on total sales), licensing can serve as a source of passive income, which is always a good thing for a freelance business.

VISUAL ARTS COPYRIGHT

Freelance creatives and entrepreneurs normally own the copyright to their work. The only requirement is that the work must not have been copied from someone else and can be proven to possess originality of expression. You can submit and file your work for copyright under the "Works of the Visual Arts" category with the U.S. Patent and Trademark Office. However, if a client commissioning work insists that the project is "for hire," then it means that the work and any copyrights are owned by the commissioning client. It's important to consider the specific work you're giving up rights to when you accept a project that is regarded as for hire. The same holds true for licensing, as oftentimes you are giving up ownership of your work once it's been licensed out.

When considering licensing your work, do your research and see what types of products and companies best fit your aesthetic. Would you love to see your patterns on bedding and wallpaper, your illustrations on greeting cards, or your hand-lettering on a premier typeface site? Or would your photos and illustrations better suit the selection available at stock image companies? If you have a unique or signature style and you want to be in control of your aesthetic and where your work appears, then handing over full rights to your work is not the best option for you. If you want to control who has the ability to use your images, be cautious with the companies you license your artwork to—are they established or a start-up? It's best to vet the company to see if it is indeed a good match for you and your work.

When approaching manufacturers that license designs, photos, or images, find the name of the art director or submissions agent and then send a letter of interest and sampling of your work in the same way that you would approach a potential client. (Some licensing companies have specific submission criteria or guidelines on their Web site.) Make sure to research what styles of illustrations, designs, or photos they typically work with, to make sure your work complements their offerings. If you are a skilled user of Photoshop, you can even create mock-ups that put your illustrations on sample items (such as a pillow, notebook, or plate), to give them an idea of what your work would look like on real products. If you choose to mail samples or a portfolio, note with the submission if what you've sent is something they can keep, or include a self-addressed stamped envelope to have it returned to you.

If a company chooses to purchase all the rights to your artwork, it means they can do whatever they want with your artwork until the end of time.

If you do obtain a licensing deal, be sure to carefully review the terms of the contract. Be clear which specific pieces of your artwork will be used, and especially where rights are transferred or retained. Educate yourself on all the specific rights that are mentioned, and if you're not comfortable reviewing the contract yourself hire an intellectual-property lawyer, who can review your contract, usually for a flat fee. Remember that designs are not copyrightable, but illustrations, film, and photographs are. If a company chooses to purchase all the rights to your artwork, it means they can do whatever they want with your artwork until the end of time.

Stock photo and illustration companies offer a range of licensing fees to a buyer on behalf of a photographer or illustrator in exchange for usage privileges or rights to an image. Prices vary depending on the size, audience, and length of use of the image. "Rights managed" stock photography offers a single licensing agreement that is negotiated for each use, whereas "royalty free" stock allows an image buyer to use the photo for an unlimited number of times for a single flat license fee. In some cases, the royalties you earn could be less than for an outright sale. In others, the opposite is true.

Another way to expose your work to licensors is to exhibit at trade shows like Surtex, PrintSource, or the International Textile Show (see Resources). At these events, you purchase booth space to show illustrations and surface patterns that you are making available for licensing or for buyers to purchase outright. This can be a way to show licensors from all over the world your work in the space of just a few days. Exposure is the biggest benefit of a trade show, as you may make connections there that you weren't able to make previously on your own.

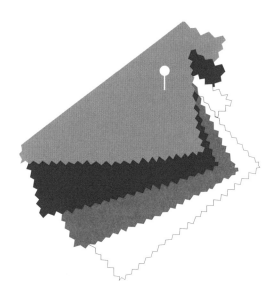

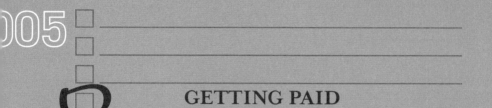

GETTING PAID

CHAPTER

5

As an artist, you may love creating your art so much, you'd do it for free. But as a business-person, you have to assign the appropriate monetary value to your time and talent, if you want your career to flourish. So what are you worth? Putting a price tag on your creative service can be unnerving. It's a pretty open-ended and objective decision, and when you're starting out it's natural to feel clueless about how much clients should pay for your work. It's normal to worry that you'll turn people off if you set your prices too high or will be giving the shirt off your back if you set them too low. This chapter takes the anxiety out of figuring out how much to charge by providing you with a simple formula to calculate your ideal hourly rate. We'll also provide advice for negotiating and estimating fees, bill-ing, managing finances, and preparing taxes—all practices you'll want to master to keep your bank balance in the black.

Putting a Price on Your Talent

In freelancing, there are two main types of fee proposals: you provide a client with an estimate for the project, or a client comes to you with a set budget for their commission. In both cases, you have to figure out the dollar amount that makes it worthwhile for you to accept the job. The trick is to strike a balance between how much you could charge and how much you should charge—all while making sure it's a reasonable price within your market. Freelancers tend to underestimate the value of their services, and only with experience, confidence, and hard-won hindsight do they gradually increase their prices. Pricing lower than the competition isn't necessarily bad if you're just out of school or are trying to build your portfolio. But once you have developed a strong body of work, it's important that your fees be commensurate with the quality you're providing. The most successful free-lancers know the value of their work and aren't afraid to stand by it.

Hourly Fee Formula

Setting an hourly fee can feel like pulling numbers out of a hat. If you recently left your full-time staff job as a Web designer, you may be inclined to use your last salary as a basis to set your new freelance hourly rate. Or, the notion of simply asking for $30 an hour may sound like a sweet deal. However, your freelance rate will likely need to be higher to cover both your personal expenses and the costs of operating a business. Using the formula on page 100, you can figure out your baseline hourly fee by first calculating the amount of gross income you need to generate per month, which includes your average monthly operating expenses, your personal expenses, estimated tax payments, and an estimate of how much money you want to reinvest in your business. You'll then determine how many days and billable hours you expect to work. You can use this baseline to set up a pricing strategy that ensures your freelance career is a lucrative pursuit.

Sample Expenses

Monthly Business Operating Expenses

Auto	$15
Travel	$45
Meals and entertainment	$50
Professional fees	$48
Dues and subscriptions	$23
Licenses and permits	$28
Insurance	$80
Marketing and promotions	$105
Internet	$20
Postage and delivery	$15
Printing and reproduction	$30
Utilities	$60
Studio rent	$490
Telephone	$40
Office supplies	$25

Total Monthly Business Expenses $1,074 (A)

Monthly Personal Expenses

Rent/mortgage	$1,000
Meals and entertainment	$240
Clothing	$180
Auto	$300
Travel	$45
Utilities	$150
Phone/Internet	$100
Credit card bills	$150
Recreational activities	$50

Total Monthly Personal Expenses: $2,215 (B)

Using the sample on the previous page, make a similar list of your business and personal expenses. Next, estimate the profit you should generate. With profit, it's good to remember that not all of your monthly profit will be take-home income; though some of it will cover your personal expenses, a good amount of it should also be reinvested in your business and placed into a savings account for quarterly taxes. Taxes will be about 25 to 48 percent of your net income (not including business expenses). We'll use 30 percent for now, but you can determine which percentage works best for you with help from a tax consultant (see Taxes, page 115).

Ideal Monthly Profit	
Total monthly personal expenses	$2,215 (B)
Business reinvestment	+ $1,200
Subtotal	$3,415
Savings for quarterly tax (est. 30% of the subtotal)	$1,024
Subtotal (above)	+ $3,415
Ideal monthly profit	**$4,439 (C)**

Gross Business Income	
Monthly business expenses	$1,074 (A)
Ideal monthly profit	+ $4,439 (C)
Total Gross Income Needed	**$5,513 (D)**

Now you have to figure out how you can make enough to cover the total monthly gross income needed. First, ask yourself two important questions: "How many days do I want to work in a month?" and "How many billable hours do I want to work in a month?" Billable hours are the time spent specifically on a client's project, for which you will be paid when the job is complete. But as you run your business, you will also have to work non-billable hours to secure new work, develop marketing plans, check e-mail, catch up on bookkeeping, or do self-initiated, portfolio-building work. It is important that you distinguish between the two. Let's say that, in the beginning, you anticipate averaging five billable hours per day and plan to work at least eighteen days per month.

Baseline Hourly Fee

Billable hours per day x Days of work per month = Total billable hours
5 hours per day x 18 days = 90 billable hours
Total gross income needed (D) ÷ Total billable hours = Hourly rate
$5,513 ÷ 90 hours = $61.25 per hour (rounded to $61 an hour)

Your formulated hourly rate is only a baseline for what your time is worth—it is not yet the magic number you will share with your clients or use to put together job proposals.

Basically, in order to cover your business and personal expenses, reinvest in your business, and save money for taxes, you'll need to bill 90 hours a month and charge a minimum of $61 an hour. Of course, this will change from month to month, but this baseline should be your minimum achievement goal. Your formulated hourly rate is only a baseline for what your time is worth—it is not yet the magic number you will share with your clients or use to put together job proposals. You still have to decide whether it's the proper amount within your field. First, you can compare it to market and industry standards within your specialty. You can check guides, such as the *Graphic Artists Guild Handbook,* that cite some standards (see Resources), or ask colleagues and mentors what the going rate is. Second, you can change the rate (overall or on a per-project basis) according to the guidelines on the following page.

Reasons to charge above your baseline fee:
- You're offering a highly specialized service for which there is very little competition.
- You have a skill set, talent, or style that has a strong following.
- You've started your freelance career after several years of experience in your industry.
- You belong to a professional guild, which can set the minimum for your services higher.
- Other comparable designers at your experience level are charging more.
- You want to market only to top-tier companies.
- The project is high in value (e.g., a logo) and will be the foundation of a buyer's business forever.
- You're working with a difficult client.
- You work very efficiently and can get the same things done in five hours that others would do in double the time.
- Your work is in high demand during certain times of the year, such as wedding season if you're a wedding photographer.

Reasons to charge at or below your baseline fee:
- You're brand new to freelancing and need portfolio-building projects.
- The project is more artistically fulfilling than usual.
- You want to get a foot in the door with a particular client.
- Your client has a set rate for all freelancers.
- For marketing purposes, you want to be the affordable option.
- Your client is a nonprofit organization or you want to add some pro bono work to your portfolio.
- The project is relatively easy or not time consuming.

Calculating by the Project

In most cases, clients prefer a set cost for a project over an open-ended one. When a project could easily span five months, clients don't want to hear your hourly rate; they want to know how much it will cost for the entire project. When you are calculating a fee for a whole project, the place to start is to make a list of all the elements involved in the project. How much research and prep time will you need? How many sketches will you show? How many rounds of revisions will be needed to get to the final result? What postproduction work is involved? Finally, will the project involve any long conference calls or travel for meetings with your client? Take account of absolutely everything you expect to come up during an assignment, so you'll avoid underselling yourself and the value of your time.

Say you've been asked to create a two-minute animation for a kids' television commercial and you typically charge $80 an hour. Your list may look something like this:

Online research on animation's subject matter:	5 hours
Storyboard sketches:	7 hours
First draft + two rounds of revisions to reach final draft:	25 hours
Postproduction editing and file formatting:	6 hours
Client meetings and travel:	3 hours
Total: 46 hours x $80 per hour =	$3,680 (baseline project rate)

Based on the suggested reasons for charging above or below your baseline hourly rate (see preceding section), you should modify your baseline project rate accordingly. For example, if you find that the industry rate for this type of project is higher than your baseline project rate, perhaps you should increase it by $500 or $1,000 to better match that standard. What's important to know is that a client does not always have to see this calculation if you choose to offer a project rate, only the final cost you'll charge. Also, because you never know exactly how many changes a customer will ask for or how drawn out the process can get, you can add a stipulation to this flat fee. You can state that the price will be $3,680 with two rounds of revisions, and any additional rounds will be billed at your rate of $80 per hour. Or, if your client isn't totally sure if the animation will need to be two or three minutes long, you can offer a range of $3,680 to $4,300 to account for the variable length, with the intention that the final price will be determined at project completion. Clients are usually okay with a range, as long as they're aware of the maximum amount they may have to pay.

If at some point during a project you realize it's taking longer than you expected (because the buyer changed his mind midway through or the details are more labor intensive than originally suggested), be sure to let him know immediately, rather than surprising him with an unexpected higher bill at the project's conclusion. Over time you may become so familiar with how long it typically takes to develop a logo, draft a chair prototype, or photograph and edit images from a day's shoot that you can offer an à la carte menu of rates for your most-called-upon services.

Estimates

Although a client may love your work, what she ultimately wants to know is "How much will it cost me?" Enter the freelancer's estimate. After you discuss the project details, you will provide the client with an estimate that not only establishes your fee but also outlines the parameters of the job and your working relationship. Avoid giving ballpark estimates, because ultimately your client will zone in on the low end of that approximation. And it should go without saying that all your business communications, including the estimate, should be professional and as accurate as possible. Typed on your letterhead, an estimate includes the following pieces:

01 Your logo and contact information

02 Date

03 Client name, address, and contact information

04 Job number or estimate number

05 Deliverables: all pieces that the client expects to have when the job is completed, as well as the specific file formats, if applicable

06 Estimated costs and fees for the project, broken down into parts if there are multiple pieces in the project

07 Any reimbursable expenses, such as travel expenses, materials puchased for the job, or meals on the day of a shoot

08 Terms: when payment is due, rush fees, cancellation policy or fees, additional fees for work beyond the agreement, permissions and ownership of work, and any other policies you have implemented with regard to payment

09 Expiration: State how long an estimate is valid. This gives potential buyers a time limit for your fees, so they don't come back a year later expecting the same pricing when your rates may have increased. Usually 30 to 90 days is an appropriate amount of time for a valid estimate.

ON THE SPOT FILMS 124 Greenwich St., New York, NY 10014
{t} 212 555 2894 {e} john@onthespotfilms.com

 September 23, 2011

 Mr. Client
246 Project Avenue
New York, NY 10013
{t} 212 555 4672
{e} client@coolcompany.com

 ESTIMATE
Estimate No: ABP01

 Client: Mr. Client, Cool Company
Designer: John Filmmaker, On the Spot Films
Project: Animation for Eco Car Commercial

Description of work (at $85/hour)
includes concepts, revisions, and final files delivered in HD
by January 4, 2012.

Sketches... 5 hours
1st round.. 20 hours
2nd round... 15 hours
Final Files.. 8 hours

TOTAL ESTIMATED HOURS.. 48 hours

TOTAL ESTIMATED COST.. $4,080.00

ADDITIONAL EXPENSES
Up to $300 additional for travel costs to Eco Car factory

TERMS
Deposit: For new clients, a non-refundable deposit of 25% of the estimated cost
is required to begin work.
Cancellation: Should the project be canceled before completion, payment will be due
for any completed work minus the deposit amount.
Payment: All invoices and any reimbursable expenses are due within 30 days
of invoice, unless otherwise discussed.
Confidentiality & Ownership: All work created for the Client and any concepts discussed
are kept confidential. Upon completion of work and payment received, the Client
owns all artwork that the Designer has created specifically for the Client.

Expiration:
The current estimate will be honored for 60 days.

Terms

Microscopic type aside, terms can be considered the "fine print" of your estimate or contract. At minimum, your terms should dictate how and when you will be paid, who has ownership of the work you've created, and what should happen if a job is canceled. Following is a look into some common factors to include in your terms on estimates and contracts.

Payment

Tell the client when payment is due. Payment within 30 days of the invoice date is most common, but you may choose to shorten (14 days) or extend (60, 90, or 120 days) the expected payment period based on the client's accounts-payable schedule. Also include payment penalty terms and the percentage service charge (usually a nominal percentage, anywhere from 1 to 5 percent) that will be applied if payment is late.

Deposit

Ask for one. A deposit can be a flat amount or a percentage of the total cost. It's due upon contract signing and should be paid before you begin any work. The deposit is deducted at the end of the project from the final fee to be paid.

Rush and additional fees

State your rush fees or additional fees up front, so the client is aware of what it will cost if he asks for quicker turnaround than your normal schedule allows or additional work beyond the agreement. You can charge a higher hourly or daily rate or add an additional percentage of the total project cost (e.g., 10 percent) onto the final bill.

Cancellation policy and kill fees

Always define what fees will be due if the job is canceled before the project is complete. Often this is based on how much work has been completed at the point of cancellation. For example, if you or a customer decides to cancel a job after you've completed 50 percent of the project, you could require 50 percent of the payment to be due as the kill fee.

Permissions and ownership

Include language about who has ownership of the completed work and when and how you and the client can use it. It's typical to state that any work files or negatives a client needs will be delivered only after final payment has been made. You can also grant yourself permission to show the work in your own portfolio or on your promotional material.

RATES AND THEIR DEFINITIONS

Day rates are most common for stylists and photographers, since it's usually impossible for them to book more than one client per day. So whether a client needs you for a three-hour shoot or a nine-hour shoot, it doesn't matter—that day is held for that client and billed at your day rate. In addition, some freelancers also offer a half-day rate to cover the prep or research time needed for the preproduction aspects of a project.

Hourly rates can be used by all freelancers, especially designers and illustrators, as a basis for all jobs and job estimates.

Flat and per-project rates provide your client with a flat fee to produce a specific project, regardless of how many hours it may take. Setting these rates does involve calculating your expected hours on a typical project, but you don't always have to inform your client of your hourly rate when you give her the total for the project.

Fee Negotiation

As mentioned previously, some clients, such as publishers, propose a fee or make an offer for your photography, styling, or illustrations. Newbie freelancers are often so anxious to get a job and develop a relationship with a client like this that they accept a lower fee just to get a foot in the door. This may become problematic, as your first contract will likely set a precedent for future jobs. There could even be text in the contract stating that this will be the contract upon which all future jobs are based, and that would be unfavorable for you. Unless the client has a rate set in stone that all freelancers must abide by, you should remember that all offers are negotiable. Likewise, in situations where you provide a client with an estimate, the client could ask you for a lower rate. Because this is a business, it's usually your client's goal to offer you the lowest competitive price for your talent and obtain the highest level of rights to your work. On the flip side, it should be your goal to obtain the highest possible fee and retain as many rights as possible.

. . . the best negotiators do more than just ask for a higher fee. They justify their request.

In negotiating, the first (and simplest) thing you can do is ask for more money or more rights. You might be surprised at the result. However, the best negotiators do more than just ask for a higher fee. They justify their request. One common justification is that the amount of effort and time involved does not match the offered compensation. As best you can, explain the work that's involved (in terms of research, time, or setup). And there's certainly an art to this delicate tug-of-war. For instance, if you can get your client to agree to a higher fee, the client may, in turn, ask you to concede some rights or may ask if they can spread payment over four months instead of two. It's a fine balance to strike, and your preferences may not be the same on every project. Just decide what's most important to you on a project-by-project basis.

As the saying goes, "Money changes everything." Thankfully, between artists and clients, it's temporary. During negotiation, remember to keep your nerves and temper in check. You want to maintain a good relationship with your client, because you certainly don't want to burn any bridges. Approach every negotiating point with confidence, a positive tone, and professionalism. Emphasize your enthusiasm and use phrases like "Can we work on that?" or "What seems like a fair amount to you?" to make it clear that you are working together toward a solution. With time and practice, your negotiating skills will get better, and you'll feel more comfortable asking for the amount you feel you are worth. But if haggling continues to be a painstaking ordeal, it may be beneficial to pass that responsibility on to someone trained for this type of negotiation, such as an agent or an intellectual-properties lawyer (see chapter 6). Not only will you dodge the awkward haggling phase of your client relationship, you'll probably score more options, rights, and money in the end.

Contracts

Once the numbers have been discussed and you and your client have agreed to the terms and set cost for the project, it's time to solidify the deal with a contract—a must for every job you take on. Whether your customer is a Fortune 500 company, a tiny mom-and-pop shop, or your aunt's best friend, every job (especially with a new client) must have an agreement in writing. Indeed, having a contract in place makes you more professional and protects you if a dispute were ever to arise. Verbal agreements will not leave you with a strong argument if you're battling over payment or deliverables. So, if your client doesn't initiate the contract, you'll need to create your own. In most cases, your proposal (job brief and estimate) can double as a contract. Simply update the cost and final delivery dates if they've changed from the original estimate. Also add spaces for the signatures of both parties, as well as the dates signed, and make sure all information on the proposal is accurate and correct. And remember: both parties have to sign in order to make the contract legally binding.

In some cases, clients will provide you with their own contract. Now, if there's any lesson to glean from the music industry, it's that you should never sign a contract in haste. As many a *Behind the Music* tale will tell us, you have to completely understand what you are signing, or you could be signing away all your rights to your work, including copyright. Don't learn this the hard way. Take out the magnifying glass, especially on the first contract, and scrutinize it properly. If the legal terminology in the contract is above your head, build or hire an army of advisers, from an intellectual-properties lawyer to freelancing peers, who can review and explain your contracts. Claiming ignorance will not get you out of a contract. The onus falls on you to protect yourself. Getting screwed on a contract may make good fodder for a celebrity backstory, but for freelancers it's better to avoid experiencing heartbreak and loss.

WORKING ON RETAINER

Are you working on an ongoing project for a theater company that has you filming its programs every month? Or has an advertising agency hired you to do animation for a string of commercials that will take more than a year to complete? If so, it may make sense for them to hire you on a retainer basis. An arrangement that will make you feel like pseudo-staff, a retainer is an agreement that includes regular payments (usually monthly) made to you by a customer who calls upon your services regularly. Retainers are a mutually beneficial arrangement: you get reliable income, and your client can spread the payments out over time. It's about as close to a steady paycheck as you'll get in freelancing. A retainer agreement can set parameters to include a certain number of hours per month, or it can be open ended to include any and all work that a client may need during the given retainer period. However, unless you can be assured that your client will not barrage you with projects, a no-limit retainer should be avoided.

When and How to Increase Fees

What you charge now is likely destined to occupy the far left spot on the evolutionary time line of your fee schedule. Your fees three, seven, or fifteen years from now will probably be different, and higher. As you gain more experience and more clients, demand for your work could increase, which means more money, but also increased expenses and overhead. You may need to move your business into a larger space outside your home or hire employees to manage the workload. You may need to hire an agent, who will get a cut of your paycheck. Your personal expenses may also deepen with marriage or the birth of children, which in turn will require you to demand a larger profit margin and more take-home pay. All this affects what you charge for your services.

You may have to explain your increased fee at times, but you should never apologize or revert back to your previous fees.

Go ahead: give yourself a raise. Although you can give yourself a standard raise of 5 or 10 percent on your fees per year, it's probably a better idea to revisit your expenses annually and recalculate your hourly fee, to make sure your raise is ample enough to cover any new or increasing expenses. And, to ensure that your fee matches your experience and reputation, consider raising your fees if you notice a growing demand for your work, as you accumulate awards and accolades, as your market shifts to higher-profile clients, or as you become a specialist in your field. It's usually not necessary to make a global announcement notifying everyone in your client database of a fee increase. You should contact only clients with ongoing jobs, who may be affected by it. Your increased fee could be a surprise to some of your clients, especially those who haven't hired you in a while. If you've really upped your rates, you can choose to offer loyal, ongoing clients a stepladder increase to ease the transition from your old rate to your new one. You may have to explain your increased fee at times, but you should never apologize or revert back to your previous fees.

Billing and Bookkeeping

Where the creative road ends for a project, a new administrative path begins. The focus at this juncture: billing and collecting. Creating an organized billing system is key to ensuring you get paid on time for the work you've been toiling over. Establish good habits early, such as sending your invoices within a week of a job's completion, to set yourself up for a predictable cash flow. Otherwise, time can slip away and invoices can start piling up. Before you know it, you'll have forgotten to bill a client for a job that finished months ago. To the right is a sample invoice to send at a project's conclusion:

01 Your logo and contact information

02 Date

03 Client name, address, and contact information

04 Job number

05 Brief description of job and deliverables

06 Final costs or fees for the project, itemized by specific charges and including any reimbursable expenses

07 Terms, including when payment is due and late fees

08 Payment information, including to whom the check should be made payable and the address to which payment should be sent. If a client asks for your social security number or EIN for tax purposes, you can include your EIN on the invoice, if you have one. Otherwise, if you're using your social security number, give it to the client's accounts-payable department separately, to avoid having such personal information on every invoice you send out.

01 ON THE SPOT FILMS 124 Greenwich St., New York, NY 10014
(t) 212 555 2894 (e) john@onthespotfilms.com

02 January 15, 2012

03 Mr. Client
246 Project Avenue
New York, NY 10013
(t) 212 555 4672
(e) client@coolcompany.com

INVOICE

04 **INVOICE**
Job No: ABP01

Client: Mr. Client, Cool Company
Designer: John Filmmaker, On the Spot Films
Project: Animation for Eco Car Commercial

05 Description of work (at $85/hour)
includes concepts, revisions, and final files delivered in HD
by January 4, 2012.

06

Sketches	6 hours
1st round	22 hours
2nd round	10 hours
Final Files	9 hours
TOTAL HOURS	47 hours
PROJECT COST	$3995.00
EXPENSES	$375.00

Rental car & gas to Eco Car factory for research and filming

TOTAL COST	$4,370.00

07 TERMS
Payment: All invoices and any reimbursable expenses are due within 30 days
of invoice, unless otherwise discussed. If payment is not received within
14 days of the due date, the Designer will not proceed with any new work
for the Client until payment has been received. The Client will also be
subject to a late fee of 5% of the amount overdue.

08 Please make payable to:
On the Spot Films
c/o John Filmmaker
124 Greenwich St.
New York, NY 10014

It's well known that organization doesn't usually rank high among creatives' many virtues. But organized accounting and business records are essential for maintaining and growing a well-operated business. The main function of record keeping is to track your invoices, payments, and expenses, all of which help to determine your "profit and loss report" every year, a necessity at tax time. You can maintain your books using old-school accounting ledgers, software such as Excel, or dedicated accounting programs such as QuickBooks or the programs available from Peachtree, which not only generate invoices but, better yet, can keep track of which ones are outstanding. If you're handling the invoices manually, be sure to log the job number and date of every invoice sent, so that you know when a payment is late and also how much income you can expect to receive over the next few months.

If you work from home, you can deduct a part of your home bills, including rent and utilities . . .

Bookkeeping also requires you to keep lots of receipts: for meals, bridge tolls, parking fees, or books you bought to research a client's industry. The minute you begin your career as a freelancer, any payments or charges you accrue solely for business purposes are considered a business expense and therefore tax deductible. That means a cab ride can be considered an expense only if you were going to your client's office, not to a friend's apartment. And just because you bought your lunch using your business credit card, that doesn't automatically make it a business expense. Any expenses that are questionable or potentially personal in nature require additional record keeping as proof of their business purpose. For business meals, write on the receipt whom you were with and the reason for the meeting. For car mileage, create a log that shows when, where, why, and how far you drove.

If you work from home, you can deduct a part of your home bills, including rent and utilities, if your office is used exclusively and regularly for business. That means your basement is tax deductible if it's used solely as your place of work, not if it also doubles as a rumpus room for your kids. As proof, you can take some digital photos and measure the space. You can then deduct a percentage of your bills based on the square footage of your home. So, if your basement is one-third of your total square footage, then one-third of your rent and utilities can be counted as business expenses.

When you're starting out, you can probably handle bookkeeping yourself to keep costs down and also to give yourself a good grasp of the financial numbers involved in running a business. Before you begin, though, it's a good idea to consult an accountant to learn some basic accounting skills, like how to set up appropriate income and expense accounts. But, at some point, if the paper shuffling becomes tedious and bean counting too time consuming, consider hiring a bookkeeper or accountant to manage your finances. Transferring this responsibility can free up time to work on other, more important aspects of your business, like connecting with clients or giving creative direction to your staff.

Taxes

Remember when you used to work for the Man? Remember those pay stubs with mysterious acronyms and tax withholdings that took a chunk out of your gross pay? You work for yourself now, but that doesn't mean all those taxes magically disappear. When you file your taxes, some of those withholdings from pay stubs past reappear in the form of the self-employment tax, or SE tax. Here, a percentage of your adjusted gross income (15.3 percent of the first $105,000 in self-employment income) is deducted to cover social security and Medicare taxes. And as a freelancer, filing taxes won't merely be a spring ritual anymore. According to the IRS, you are required to pay state and federal taxes quarterly—which could mean, if your business is earning a profit, tax payments four times a year. Learning to put money aside will be critical, so you won't find yourself scrounging to make these tax payments.

Tax paperwork can also come from your clients. They may ask you to fill out a W-9, or a Request for Taxpayer Identification Number and Certification, either before the project begins or when you send them your first invoice. The W-9 asks for your social security number (if you're a sole proprietor) or your EIN (if you decide to get one). At the end of the year, your client will generate a 1099 form (a tax document reporting a business trans-action) indicating how much they paid for your services that year. A copy of this will be sent to you usually by January 30 of the following year. You should reconcile your 1099s with your invoice records to double check your record keeping. Likewise, if you paid any independent contractors, such as a photographer's assistant, you should provide them with a 1099 as well.

After five years of working full-time for larger firms and spending their weekends doing taxes for friends (and friends of friends), most of whom were tax challenged and disorganized musicians and artists, it occurred to Alyssa and Mark Fox that there was a need for tax consultation and preparation among creatives. In 2004, they self-published the *Creative Tax Planner*, and in the following year they launched Fox Tax Service in Minneapolis, catering primarily to creative-business owners—a niche market that reflected both their talents and their interests. In five years, they've gone from a few friends to more than 2,500 clients, the majority of whom are in a creative field. Although they started their business in their home, they now operate from a warehouse in the Arts District of northeast Minneapolis. Dedicated to serving and promoting artists, they reserve some of their office space for a curated gallery where they showcase the artwork of a different client every few months.

When it comes to record keeping, what's a common problem you see among creative businesses?

Creatives often lack a record-keeping system altogether. For them, it's about finding motivation. Business owners should treat a ten-dollar receipt like a real ten-dollar bill—that type of perspective shift is usually helpful. I also like to suggest that business owners file their receipts by categories rather than by month. At the end of the year (and if you are audited), the expenses need to be sorted and tallied by groupings of type rather than by date, so it's easier to do this during the year as you go, rather than years later, when they are all faded.

Can you tell us more about paying taxes quarterly?

Paying taxes quarterly refers to making estimated payments toward your annual tax bill. Essentially, the IRS would like those with profitable businesses or other untaxed sources of income to send in taxes as they earn the income, just like having it taken out of a paycheck. So "filing quarterly" refers to sending in a check each quarter—on April 15, June 15, October 15, and January 15—as an estimate of what you will owe at year-end. If your tax bill is over $1,000 for the year, then, yes, you should pay quarterly, as the IRS may impose penalties if you did not mail in payments on a quarterly basis. Penalties are calculated per day and usually come up to 3 to 4 percent of the total due. If it's your first year of business, there is a good chance that estimated taxes are not necessary; expenses are usually higher in start-up businesses, which lowers the tax and may keep it under $1,000 for the year.

How would you suggest estimating how much to put aside for quarterly taxes?

When estimating taxes, the IRS would like you to estimate 90 percent of your current tax bill, or you can base it on 100 percent of the prior year's tax bill. The actual amount differs for everyone, of course, based on your income for the year and how much you have in expenses, as well as if you're filing individual or jointly. Generally, an average of 25 to 48 percent of your net business income becomes tax. So depending on the size of your income, you should plan accordingly. With my clients, I try to emphasize that the tax can be close to 50 percent of your income, which makes keeping track of business expenses extremely valuable.

Do you have any advice for freelancers on starting a retirement savings plan?

There are many different options for retirement plans. Choosing the right one for you depends on age, income level, and the amount that you want to put in savings each year. If you are younger, make under $100,000 per year, and would like to save under $5,000 per year for retirement, then a Roth IRA is a great type of account. The money grows tax free and has fewer penalties if you need to access it early. If you want to save more than $5,000 per year or your income exceeds $100,000, then you may need a different type of retirement account. A newer type of retirement account is a Roth 401(k), which is available to a sole proprietor as well as to company employees. If you are the only person involved in your plan, then fees are relatively cheap. This allows you to put up to $16,000 into a Roth account, plus you can put up to 20 percent of self-employed earnings (after expenses) into a tax-deductible account. It's like having two retirement accounts in one plan: one that is deductible now and taxable later, and one that is not deductible now, but tax free later.

CHAPTER

6

AGENTS

An agent can change your freelance career. She can make connections and create opportunities that might be difficult for you to score on your own, such as hooking you up for a photography assignment with a major computer company or illustrating a children's book by a celebrity author. Not only can having an agent help you land these elusive clients, it also can help you develop your talent and increase the value of your work—in return for a commission, of course. Though giving away a chunk of your pay is difficult, the payoff is having someone who finds you new work, implements marketing plans, negotiates your contracts for you, and bills and collects payments from clients—all so that you can concentrate on your art. In this chapter, we'll talk about whether an agent is right for you, what it's like to work with an agent, how to find one who is best for you, and, in case your agent doesn't turn out to be a good match or provide what you expected, how to end the relationship.

Is an Agent Right for You?

Just because everyone and her mother has an agent in the writing and entertainment industries, it doesn't mean that getting an agent is right for you. Not everyone needs to or wants to work with an agent. Some fields, like graphic design, are rarely represented by agents, whereas in other fields, like illustration, you'll find a mixed bag of agented and nonagented artists. If you decide to work without an agent, the obvious benefit is keeping 100 percent of your profits. And if you enjoy working with clients and vendors one on one, a solo path allows you to make connections and form relationships directly with art directors and editors, which is an invaluable experience. When you bring in jobs on your own, you're in control and free to work with whom you want, when you want. Plus, you'll reap all the rewards with the satisfaction of knowing you did it all by yourself.

. . . if the thought of e-mailing editors and art directors cold makes you break out into a cold sweat, then seeking out an agent may be a good move.

Truly, no one can represent you better than yourself. Only you know the direction you want your business to go and which projects will take you there. Basically, you know what is most important to you. If an agent represents you, can you be assured your agent has your best interests in mind, or could he be merely pursuing projects on your behalf that support his bottom line? How will you know if your agent will secure jobs that will stimulate your creative talent? Would it be okay if he passed over a creatively strong (albeit lower-paying) book project to pursue a higher-paying (albeit creatively dull) advertising project? As you can see, when you have someone representing you, trust and communication become very important in maintaining a good relationship. You have to clearly communicate your objectives to your agent and trust that he will act responsibly on your behalf. Because your agent is an extension of yourself, many of his actions—in particular, poor ones—can reflect back on you. If you are not willing to relinquish control of your career and put this type of decision-making power in someone else's hands, then getting an agent may not be right for you.

Then again, if the thought of e-mailing editors and art directors cold makes you break out into a cold sweat, then seeking out an agent may be a good move. While they can certainly become successful on their own, some freelancers (especially film directors, photographers, stylists, and illustrators) choose to work with an agency or representative to give them more exposure than they might be able acquire on their own. The biggest advantage to having an agent is his connection with clients—agents know their buyers well and interact with them regularly. If it's an established agency, they've spent years cultivating their client database, which means they could get you access to high-profile clients that would be difficult to court independently. Some agents have connections with advertising agencies that represent high-end clients with five- or six-digit budgets, making your current gig's fees look like bake-sale money. With these established client relationships, an agent can speak about your potential freely and easily, rather than you having to talk yourself up to a stranger. The agent puts your work in front of a customer's eyes without you having to make that connection on your own. In this way, you could quickly land a major contract that would instantly propel your career to a whole new level.

In your search for an agent, it's often helpful to find someone who's been in your shoes before. Indeed, Lilla Rogers, an artist-turned-agent, understands the practical and emotional issues that artists often experience. An accomplished illustrator herself, Lilla has seen her work grace the pages of the *New York Times*, not to mention having scored commissions from Barneys and Levi-Strauss. She stumbled into being an agent while she was teaching from her studio. Juggling a freelance career and teaching, she started receiving more illustration work than she could handle. So she began passing the jobs on to her most talented students. They, in return, begged her to represent them. And thus, the Lilla Rogers Agency was born in 1994. Even now, Lilla continues to mentor her current crop of illustrators, teaching classes and workshops filled with advice grounded in her own experience. For Lilla Rogers, representing artists means more than just a paycheck; it embodies her commitment to her artists' growth and development.

Where did you get the idea to teach classes to your artists? What topics do you cover?

We are a very community-minded agency. Our agency's goal is more than just to represent artists, but to foster their growth as well. I wanted to have classes to help our artists evolve and stay fresh and relevant. I like to customize the classes to the artists, and we offer both individual and group instruction. For the group classes, the artists come from across the country, so it's great that they get to meet each other in person. I teach classes like how to prepare for trade shows like Surtex and PrintSource or how to create illustrations that are more editorially fresh. The classes often take place over the span of five weeks. When we get together, I feel like I'm teaching a super-gifted class, so it's a tremendous pleasure to teach them.

How many submissions do you get every year? How do you go about selecting an artist for your agency?

We get about a thousand submissions every year. Selecting an artist is part brain, part gut. First of all, I must really love her work. The artist must be very gifted, have a strong aesthetic, and appear as though she is having fun with her work. I also have to be able to envision where her work would fit: editorial or scrapbooking or something else. If she sends me an e-mail, it needs to be intelligent, organized in thought, and have a sense of warmth. When sending an e-mail to a prospective agent, think of it like wearing your best outfit to a job interview. The e-mail should also have about five images attached and include a link to your Web site. When I visit an artist's Web site, the personality of her work has to be evident. I'll sometimes stay around on the site for two to three clicks, so if she has a slow-loading Web site or if it just looks tacky, it's a turnoff.

As a team, we look at the top submissions we receive. We'll flag a few that we find incredible and file them in a folder. The process can take over a year from when an artist sends his submission to actually signing with the agency. So, if he doesn't hear back from us, we suggest that the artist keep sending us his work. Sometimes we love an artist but we're so busy that getting through to us comes down to persistence and timing.

If we are considering an artist, we may ask her to send printed pieces for review. We also consider if she has other promotional avenues, like whether she has a blog or an Etsy site. We then have a staff meeting to get everyone's reaction. I should note, in rare cases, there are times when we have gone after an artist who hasn't approached us first.

Do you prefer artists who have more experience?

It's fun sometimes to take on a brand-new discovery. Even if they're new, they need to show a high level of professionalism.

With regard to territory, do you represent your artists internationally or just in the United States? Do you ever accept any international artists?

Territorially, we represent the artists internationally. However, for artists abroad, we normally allow them to have their home countries—that is, they can get jobs that originate from their home countries without having to go through our agency. They could even have another agent in their country representing them.

We have a very aggressive promotion program. We handle it all for our artists, as we don't want them to spend time dealing with the business end of things. We just want them to focus on producing good work. We also exhibit at trade shows like Surtex. At the beginning of each year, we give each artist an à la carte menu of marketing options, from being included in postcard mailings to participating in Surtex. Because we work in a large group, we're able to offer our artists various options for their marketing at a more reasonable rate than if they took these opportunities on their own.

The Benefits of Having an Agent

An agent is typically responsible for showcasing your work to potential clients, devising and executing marketing plans, landing you jobs, negotiating the terms for every contract, and handling the billing and payment processes. In some ways, an agency offers a guaranteed support team, much like you'd have with a full-time employer, only without the nine-to-five hours. The agency takes on the minutiae of administrative tasks, manages client relationships, seeks out new markets, and vets clients on their suitability. In return, agents receive a commission that may range anywhere from 15 to 50 percent of each job. A common commission for photography and styling reps is 15 to 25 percent, while licensing reps charge upward of 50 percent. Some agents have a flat-rate commission, some have a tiered commission system, and others charge different fee levels depending on your type of work. In all cases, commissions are never paid up front. Agents take a commission from your earnings only after you are paid.

Fee negotiations are often better handled by a third party, because it can be tricky to manage a good relationship with a client while simultaneously being a tough negotiator.

In addition to bringing in new business and having years of experience in the industry, agents understand contracts and negotiating. This might be an area that feels foreign to you, but all the technical writing and legalese in contracts concerning options, rights, subrights, usage rights, and exclusivity is second nature to them. Fee negotiations are often better handled by a third party, because it can be tricky to manage a good relationship with a client while simultaneously being a tough negotiator. Agents are able to negotiate in your favor without the emotional attachment you may feel when discussing the worth of your own work. Because new artists most likely will not know what the market rate is or what other artists have been paid, agents often can secure them better fees, knowing the going rate and history of what certain clients can pay. Agents know the value of both your work and the project at hand and can confidently ask for two, three, four, or even ten times the amount that a client might be offering you, whereas you might have trouble demanding that sort of fee. Agents may also be able to get you multiple contracts and more options than you could secure on your own.

There is a certain vulnerability that comes with being an unrepresented artist. If you are part of an agency, you have the strength of a group on your side. On the off chance that you have a troublesome client and are having problems getting paid, it is less likely that the client will want to risk losing the potential of working with a whole roster of artists. Moreover, there is a certain cachet to having an agent. Telling a potential client that you have an agent or announcing it on your Web site gives the impression that you are in demand, a sought-after artist. And aligning yourself through association with other respected artists on your agent's roster can legitimize or even raise your status among your peers and in the eyes of potential clients. For example, if the agency itself has a reputation for finding the next big artist, it can instantly put your name on a client's radar.

Most people think of having an agent just as a means of getting steady work, almost like having an employer. Especially for new college grads or green artists, having an agent can lend a sense of security in the face of leaving a structured environment to manage a freelance career. But you should be realistic about what an agent can do for you. An agent may not spoon-feed you a continuous stream of projects. And, even though your agent may get you jobs, it's up to you to execute each one properly and keep the clients coming back for more.

Finding an Agent

Agencies vary in what they look for. Some agencies choose to work only with established artists. It can sometimes take years to hone an artistic vision, so these agents may prefer an artist with a clear style and some experience under her belt, someone who is already reputable and saleable. Other agents may be trying to find groundbreaking talent to bring into the marketplace. They may take a proactive approach, eyeing the homegrown art scene on blogs or seeking out budding artists at graduation shows. So if you are a recent grad, know that some agents will not pick you up simply because of your newness to the trade. In cases where you have reached the peak of your success and have developed a solid following, know that agents may come after you at a time when you might feel like you don't really need one.

As you seek out an agent, remember that the most important thing agents look for in an artist is someone who creates marketable work and who has a strong sense of his own work style. According to the New York–based agent Sarah Laird, "Photographers and stylists should avoid shooting what they think will get them a job. They should stick to their style. When they meet with a rep, they should be clear about who they are, where they are, and what their brand is. For photographers, I look for great pictures and a good personality. For stylists, I look for a great sense of style and someone who is super organized. The artists should be proactive and be knowledgeable about themselves as well as the business they're in."

Look for an agent who is a good fit with your aesthetic, with whom you feel your artwork will thrive, and who is with an agency you'd be proud to call your own.

Remember: you don't want to be represented by just anyone. Not all agents are the same, so you must choose wisely. Look for an agent who is a good fit with your aesthetic, with whom you feel your artwork will thrive, and who is with an agency you'd be proud to call your own. Start your search by looking for names of agents on the Web sites of artists you respect (they normally list their agent with their contact information) or in annuals featuring the year's best illustrators or photographers. Ask fellow artists for feedback on their agents or for any bits of information they've heard about specific agents working in your field. Word travels fast about artist-agent relationships, both good and bad. Always look at the other artists an agent represents to be sure your work could comfortably coexist and, most important, would not compete with or look too similar to the work of the artists on the roster. In other words, you need to simultaneously fit in and stand out. Also, take inventory of an agency's client list—how many notable clients does it have that would be difficult for you to get on your own? What is the agency culture like? Look at how many agents it has on staff and how many artists they represent—do you feel like you'll get enough personal attention, or will you get lost in the crowd? Gauge an agent's familiarity with and experience in the industry by asking how long the agency has been around, and try to find out more about the agent's background.

After you've narrowed down your search to a few agents you feel would be the best fit, start with your first choice and work your way down the list. Check out the agency Web site for its submission policy and follow the guidelines to a T. If there are no guidelines, send an e-mail asking what the agency's preference is: submission by e-mailed PDF, online portfolio link, or physical portfolio mailed to them. Remember, some of the more popular agents receive more than a thousand submissions per year, so it can take a while to wade through the slush pile of submissions received. If an agency shows interest, try to arrange a face-to-face meeting. In a time of endless anonymous communication, meeting in person could help you make a strong impression. You will be spending a lot of time interacting with your agent, so it's the perfect opportunity to make sure you have a good rapport and feel confident in the agent's ability to foster this potential new business relationship. In the end, it is all about trust and having a good feeling that the agent will represent you, your work, and your interests in the best way possible.

Be sure to read the fine print, ask questions, and never sign the contract in haste.

When you have found an agent to represent you, she'll present you with a contract. The contract will provide a description of the working relationship, the agent's commission rates, and the terms of the agreement. Be sure to read the fine print, ask questions, and never sign the contract in haste. If you're unsure, you can always have an intellectual-property lawyer review the contract on your behalf. Be very aware of the agency's terms and policies. For instance, what happens in the event you decide to leave the agency? What's the time frame of the contract, and do you have an option to renew the contract? To eliminate any surprises down the road, be sure to inquire about additional costs you could incur, such as charges for sending and returning your portfolio to clients, having a page on the agency's Web site, using portfolio sleeves with the company's emblem, or any promotional costs for annuals or postcards. Ask if larger costs, such as for promotional materials, need to be paid up front or if they can work out a payment plan.

When you sign with an agent, you will be tied to that agency for a period of time (usually a year or two to start), and you must do work exclusively through them in the area they represent. All agents cover a specific territory (the United States, North America, South America, Asia, Europe, etc.), so artists can have several agents covering different territories. But before you go out and seek multiple agents, it's best to run the idea by your current agent, to make sure you won't be stepping on any toes. Even if a potential client contacts you directly, you will ultimately have to refer him back to the agency in the proper territory to request more details about your work. Artists must honor the agreement with their agent, as failure to do so will be deemed a breach of the contract. If you are a well-established artist joining an agency, you might be able to keep a list of clients outside of the agency. Check with the agent to see what the policy is on this. Ultimately, the agent-artist relationship must be built on mutual trust and respect, if the relationship is to flourish.

The path to self-discovery, as Nina Chakrabarti learned, isn't always as straight as an arrow. After receiving an undergraduate degree from Central Saint Martins in graphic design (focusing on illustration), the Calcutta native spent the following seven years at odd jobs such as working at a college art shop and serving as a bartender while freelancing on the side. Serendipity struck while she was collaborating with an animator on a music video project and it inspired her to go back to graduate school for animation at the Royal College of Art in London. However, she didn't find true passion in animation and instead rediscovered her love of illustration. But even with a master's degree in hand, she found that positions for staff illustrators were few and far between. Freelancing full-time became her only alternative. Agent free and proud of it, Nina has, over the years, pulled in clients like Habitat, Penguin Books, HarperCollins, Nike, Topshop, *Harper's Bazaar*, and *Vogue*. Now, finding a quiet moment isn't easy for the fifteen-year illustration veteran. Nina's story demonstrates that dabbling in a little bit of everything is a good way to test the creative waters. But in the end, subscribing to the feng shui idea of keeping only what you truly love is the key to happiness.

Who was your first client, and how did you land that job?

My first client was French Connection, which I was thrilled to get. I was commissioned to come up with a logo for their cafe and to do some illustrations to be used on their windows and walls. I landed that through a friend of mine who was working for a design company that was doing all their branding and signage at the time. I enjoyed the job a lot, but, in hindsight, I could have done a better job staying in touch with them afterward, to stay current in their minds for more projects in the future.

What made you decide not to work with an agent? Have you ever considered working with one?

I considered working with one in the past. However, the agents I've approached have not been interested in representing me, and the agents that have approached me didn't feel like a good fit. It never worked out, as a consequence. At first I used to hate negotiating my contracts, but I've become used to it and have grown to like the feeling of control it gives me. I can't imagine having an agent now.

Do you use any strategies for negotiating for better pay and rights?

I don't have a specific strategy; it depends a lot on the project and client. When I left college, I didn't have a clue about pay, copyright, or rights. I just learned things along the way. Now I either have a daily rate or I work within a project's budget. The good thing is, you get better at gauging what your rate should be or what you think you should be getting for a certain job with time and experience. Of course there will be a back-and-forth when people want to haggle you down. Although I'm open to negotiating, if I really don't want to work beneath a certain price I'll just hold my ground. And never be too desperate! If they want you, they will pay and agree to your terms. And if not, I've learned it wasn't meant to be.

How do you find interesting work, or does it find you usually? Do you do any promotional activity for your work?

I find that when I make personal work that I find interesting, that's when the great jobs come a-knockin'. I think it is important to keep developing your own work separate from financial and commercial restraints. It is imperative to create a space for yourself where you can be more experimental and explore personal themes. I don't do any promotional activity apart from having a Web site that I send out to all my previous clients, art buyers of advertising agencies, and publishing houses and magazines with whom I'm interested in working.

Do you have any tips for time management and how to get things done when you're working independently?

Just don't overload yourself. Don't say yes to things when you know you really don't have the time to fit it in. I estimate how long projects will take and often add a day or so, just in case they take longer than expected. Of course, sometimes things are too good, well paying, or exciting to turn down. In which case you should be organized, don't get drunk the night before you have to hand in work, and try to be systematic about what needs to be done. I also try to clean my desk at the end of each day, as I find working in a messy space really distracting.

I share a studio in Borough, a neighborhood in London, with a few designers, a photographer, another illustrator, and a fashion stylist. What I enjoy most is the convivial atmosphere that exists in the studio. We are all friends, which makes for a good working environment. Also, when I'm having a hard time deciding if an illustration is working or not, it's very helpful to be able to ask my studiomates what they think. I always value their opinion, and it can speed up the creative process. Sometimes, though, it does get noisy, which is hard when I need peace and quiet. I wish I had a switch I could press which would give me total silence when I need it.

What's next for you and your career?

Last year, I wrote and illustrated my first book. It's an activity book for young girls called *My Wonderful World of Fashion*. It was my dream job to complete, and I hope to do more of the same in the future. I'm also working on a fully illustrated cookbook for kids, which would be another dream job if it gets published.

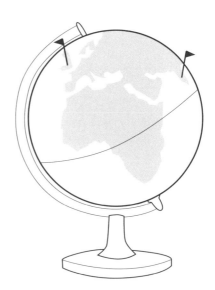

Working with an Agent

The agent-artist dynamic can be an interesting one. Many artists desperately seek an agent, only to then focus on the negatives once they've secured a rep. So, before signing, it's best to understand what agents do (and, specifically, what they can do for you), so that you can better appreciate the role they play in your career. The best agents are equal parts cheerleader and mentor, giving you insider information on how the industry works as well as advice to help you develop as an artist. Though they are providing you with a service, the benefits of that service won't always be obvious on every commission. Agents who take on new artists may need to spend more time developing and promoting them before the artists see the work pour in. It is not solely your work that will get you places—all the legwork and connections made behind the scenes are what really make it all happen. It's best to think of your relationship as one of a team working in unison toward the same goals.

Generally, potential buyers contact an agent to see which artists might fit their needs for something like an upcoming ad campaign, photo shoot, or book cover. Agents attend client meetings that are either speculative or for a specific project. During the speculative meetings, they often bring along the portfolios of specific artists, if the client has expressed interest in any, as well as a group book featuring work by their entire roster. Agents are responsible for matching a client's needs with artists in their roster who might be suitable. So as a client looks through the books, agents take notes of the client's interest and arrange to send individual portfolios later (if they are not on hand). For meetings that discuss a specific project, the artist may be asked to be present (virtually or in person). Artists often speak directly with the client about the project's specifics only after the fees and contracts have been settled. At that point, an agent typically steps aside and lets the artist work through the project with the client. In rare instances, some agents are ever present, acting as the gatekeeper so the client and artist don't communicate directly. But, more so these days, clients and artists speak to each other openly.

Ending an Agent Relationship

An agent has the capability to be your biggest supporter and get you dream jobs you never thought you'd land. But depending how things go, you may find yourself not meshing with your agent, not getting much more work than when you were pursuing projects on your own, or finding you really miss direct client interaction. Try to discuss any fixable issues with your agent first, to see if your concerns can be resolved. If you're simply ready to move on, do your best to finish out your contract, to avoid burning bridges. Your agent will likely understand that you've decided to find a new rep who is a better fit or that you've decided being agented just isn't for you. If you can't bear to wait out the remaining time on your contract, read over your termination clause and see what fees you'll incur by ending your contract early. In the end, the choice is yours. You need to surround yourself with the best team of people possible to expand and steer your business in the direction of your choosing.

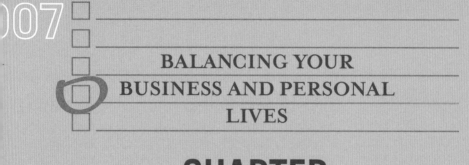

BALANCING YOUR
BUSINESS AND PERSONAL
LIVES

CHAPTER

7

Studio space? Check. Web site? Check. Clients? Check. Life . . . What? With any luck, you've got a constant stream of patrons knocking on your door, and you're working more hours than ever. You're probably so busy, you hardly notice the swift march of time. But when you find yourself often working in isolation to meet a rash of deadlines with daylight quickly fading, it's important to remember how your social and family life may also be fading. Skipping the occasional family dinner or missing a friend's birthday can quickly snowball into a bad habit of overprioritizing your work life. Setting goals and efficient work habits and allowing yourself more "me time" will keep the "workaholic" label at bay. More important, you won't slight the relationships that matter most when both your business and personal lives share a healthy and happy coexistence.

Goal Setting

Freelancing allows you to shape your career as you go along, but it's easy to get caught up with the day-to-day tasks and miss the bigger picture. How will you know what's in the future if you're always working facedown at the keyboard? Every once in a while, step away from the spate of tasks at hand to set some goals. And these goals don't have to be all about business. To get a handle on developing that work-life balance, your goals could be infused with elements that are equal parts business and personal. Where do you want to be, and what lifestyle do you want to have six months, one year, or five years from now? To begin brainstorming, ask yourself the following questions:

01 How many hours do I want to work per week?

02 How much free time do I want?

03 How much money do I want to make? What do I want my rates to eventually be?

04 What types of clients do I want that I don't already have?

05 Do I want to focus on any specialty within my trade, or do I want to broaden my services?

06 How can I earn more passive income?

07 Should I hire additional help, such as an intern, assistant, or a full-time employee?

08 How many vacations do I want to take?

09 What will I be doing to make sure that I am physically active?

10 How many social and cultural activities do I want to attend regularly?

After you've thought about some goals, break them down into small, achievable stages. Let's say you have a goal of taking at least a one-month vacation every year. In what ways can you fund that vacation? Perhaps you'll decide to generate additional income by moving from traditional illustration into animation. In the following example, we show you how you take an end goal and work backward.

One-year goal: Create animations for a top animation studio.

Nine months: Sign on with animation studio for a variety of freelance projects.

Six months: Submit my portfolio to the studio at the top of my list. Move down the list if the first studio doesn't have interest.

Two months: Find out contact information and submission guidelines for each studio. Edit and tighten my portfolio to highlight work that is most relevant to my selected studios. Create self-initiated projects if applicable work doesn't already exist on my Web site.

One month: Make a list of studios that may be interested in my aesthetic.

One week: Ask colleagues and do research online to find animation studios that work with freelancers regularly.

Working Smart

Good time management and discipline are the calling cards of a well-balanced freelancer. It's easy to fall into certain work habits without realizing that there may be more efficient ways of doing things. Ask more seasoned freelancers about their work habits and adopt processes that will increase your productivity. Over time, revisit your work practices—as your clients and lifestyle change, so should your work habits. You might need to change your routine to add variety to your day, or vice versa: insert structure into your day if it's too loose. Remember that efficiency can also open up more downtime for you. Following are some tips for working smart and improving your work routine:

Keep a calendar

This may seem obvious, but organized scheduling is a must. Because your workload may vary from day to day and week to week, it's important to plan ahead whenever possible. Break down the parts of every project and track what needs to be accomplished on a daily, weekly, and monthly basis. When other opportunities arise, you'll be less inclined to overbook yourself.

Establish daily routines and habits

If you find yourself working at random or irregular times, consider trying to stick to a daily start and end time. You don't have to follow typical nine-to-five hours, but establishing a general beginning and end to your workday will impose a better sense of urgency on completing all your required tasks before your "work" hours are over. You can designate certain hours of the day for checking e-mail and returning voice-mail messages, since these tasks can be huge distractions that cut into your flow. It's also helpful to develop habits for routine tasks, such as sending out invoices the day you finish a job or paying all your bills on the first day of every month.

Track your time

Use online time-tracking tools (see Resources) to record the amount of time you spend on every project. Not only will this be helpful for invoicing and creating future estimates, but it will also help you be as efficient as possible by showing you how much time you're really spending on each assignment.

Separate work and home

When you work from home, create boundaries so that your work space is as separate as possible. Whether your studio is in a different room or marked off by a room divider, a physical boundary defines where your work area is and encourages you to stay out of that space during your time off. If you can avoid home activities like watching TV, reading magazines, or doing the laundry, you're less likely to get sucked in by non-work-related diversions. Also, getting dressed in the clothes you'd wear if you were heading to the office can put you in work mode. You don't have to put on a fancy suit or dress, but it helps to be more productive if you're not in your pajamas all day.

Invest in tools to increase your productivity

Maybe you've been saving up for that large-format printer (because you're on a first-name basis with the employees at Kinko's) or eyeing that sleek ergonomic desk chair (because your kitchen-cum-office chair is killing your back). Make smart decisions and buy new equipment only when it's sure to benefit your working conditions and increase your productivity.

Take breaks

When you're working solo, it can be very easy for your workaholic sensibilities to take over. Before you know it, you're working through lunch, into the wee hours of the morning, and even on the weekends. By taking breaks, you'll be less likely to procrastinate and will feel more recharged to dive back in to work. So, whenever possible, meet up with other people for lunch, go get that afternoon latte, create a ten-minute yoga routine, or simply force yourself to step away from your desk or go outside for a breath of fresh air every few hours.

THE FREELANCE PARENT

Freelancing has the potential to offer the perfect balance between keeping your career and being a full-time parent. But be warned: while you can certainly save money on child care by being home for your children, it can prove difficult to conduct business while your kids are just in the other room. Most clients will not be understanding about the loud shrieks of sibling rivalry breaking out in the background, and you can easily get distracted when your four-year-old tugs on your sleeve asking for lunch in the middle of a conference call. The most effective way to balance both is to set aside certain days or hours of the day when you can work child free. Whether your kids are in school, at your parents' house, or taking their daily nap, you should put aside time to work when they're otherwise occupied. You know your family's schedule best, so keep it in mind when planning your workload and taking on clients whose demand may conflict with your at-home responsibilities.

For Ward Jenkins, freelancing became an unexpected career. In 2007, he moved his family cross-country from Atlanta, Georgia, to Portland, Oregon, to take a new job as an animation director. Within fourteen months of his arrival, he was laid off. With a wife and two young children to support, he was initially fearful of embracing the instability of self-employment. He may not have realized it at the time, but everything he had accomplished in his career to that point would ease the transition into freelancing. He had worked in the animation industry for more than twelve years and had developed many contacts and friendships. And he had already made a name for himself in the blog world. Clearly, Ward was ahead of the game. What seemed like a sour turn of events yielded great results in the end. Freelancing has given Ward the opportunity to seek dream projects and increase the quality of his personal life at the same time. Thanks to his self-employed status, he's been able to check two major goals off his list: illustrating a children's book and spending more time with his family.

What other companies had you worked for full time before freelancing? What made you decide to try freelancing?

I had been working full time since 1996. The design and animator directors from Design EFX, where I had interned, started a new satellite office called Click 3X. They had a national spot airing and needed people right away. They hired me full time to do hand-drawn 2-D animation and luckily they gave me a lot of leeway to do my own thing. It was great, because the directors were also a part of the local chapter of ASIFA [Association Internationale du Film D'Animation or the International Animated Film Society], so I also helped out with their events and had the chance to show my demo reel during event screenings.

After working four years at Click 3X, I moved on to Primal Screen in Atlanta as an animation director. Then, in 2007, I took a job with Laika in Portland, Oregon, as their animation director. My wife, two kids, our cat, and I drove across the country for this new opportunity. I worked on projects like a commercial for Cookie Crisp. But not too long after I got there, I was laid off for economic reasons.

The layoff was scary. I was so used to having a full-time job, paid health care, and the security of a steady paycheck to support my family. Being let go at Laika was an eye-opener for me. I tried to find jobs, but they just weren't available. I thought about freelancing, but I was definitely afraid of the instability. My wife and I had a powwow and decided I should try and make a go at freelancing. That pivotal discussion really helped, and I was able to relax a bit after that.

What were the first steps you took when you decided to go freelance?

Because I was let go so suddenly, I had to frantically revamp my portfolio and demo reel and put together a Web site really quickly. And then it dawned on me that I could ask for help in my time of need. So I started calling people, like previous clients and old coworkers, to inform them of my freelance status and ask them if they had any jobs that would be a good fit for me. Within several weeks, I was working on a commercial spot for the Saatchi and Saatchi ad agency. I had done work for them previously at Laika and Primal and had become good friends with the creative director.

When did you start your blog, Ward-O-Matic? Has it been helpful in getting you jobs as well?

I started the blog in 2004, while I was working at Primal. I mostly post about things that I like and find inspiring. I'm a big collector of old children's books and interesting things from the '50s and '60s. I now have a pretty good following on the blog. Since 2005, I've also been a part of a multiauthor blog called Drawn! There are eight contributing bloggers within the United States, Canada, and Australia. The guy who started Drawn! and I had a mutual appreciation for each other's blogs, so he invited me to join as a contributing blogger. I think having a presence among blogs has certainly helped me, as a lot of people know me that way. Back then, I had also started a Flickr account where I posted a lot of my work, and it became a makeshift portfolio. Since then I've created a real Web site. It's essential to have your own organized site, as it makes it easier for art directors and book publishers to view your work, and it looks much more professional.

I love that I get to do the things that I've always dreamt of doing but never had the time for when I worked full time as a director. I had always dreamt about illustrating a children's book. After I launched my freelance site, Simon and Schuster called, asking if I would illustrate a children's book with celebrity author Michael Phelps. I couldn't believe I was being paid to do what I had always wanted to do!

The biggest benefit of being a freelancer, though, is having more time to spend with my family. I don't have to ask for the day off to go on vacation or hang out with my kids. I used to come home every day for lunch, and now I'm here every day all day long.

It's a challenge to juggle both, for sure. But it's certainly made it easier for Andrea, my wife, now that I'm around. Andrea is also a freelance writer and photographer, so we trade off with the babysitting. That's the great advantage to being home. Now the kids can see their Daddy more and Mom can work on other things. When you have kids, you have to find windows of opportunity to work. Since they're in grade school, it gives us a couple solid hours a day to do some work. I'm also a night owl, so I do work a lot at night, and that way I can take advantage of my time with them during the day.

With kids, you have to set boundaries. When I'm downstairs, they know I can't be interrupted. I do let them know when I have to go downstairs to work, and they know that I always come up for lunch. I don't want to stay holed up in the basement working all day, and I don't want the kids to wonder why they never see Dad even though he's in the house. So you just have to find a balance with everything. Being at home with my family and being able to help out more has been great for us. I feel like I've become a better person, both emotionally and creatively. ✦

Dealing with Creative Blocks

You know the feeling: staring at a blank page or a blank screen, waiting for that creative epiphany to strike. Creative blocks happen to everyone. And they can feel immobilizing, especially when you're in the business of coming up with new ideas. When creative blocks happen frequently in tandem with a sense of mental or physical exhaustion, it may be creative burnout. It's probably a sign that you need rest, a change of pace, and a new point of view to get those creative juices flowing again. Bear in mind that this is just a temporary state of being, and there is probably an enormous well of energy just waiting to be rediscovered. There are lots of simple ways to get yourself out of this funk and spring back to your usual self.

While your studio may normally be your go-to place to conduct business, spark inspiration by working somewhere else for the day.

A change of scenery can often revive you when you're in a creative slump. While your studio may normally be your go-to place to conduct business, spark inspiration by working somewhere else for the day. Take your laptop to the local coffee shop, take your camera to the park, or bring your sketchbook to the museum. You can also take small steps to refresh your surroundings by rearranging your inspiration board, changing the art on your walls, or moving your desk from one side of the room to another. Supplement these physical tweaks to your routine with cerebral explorations by learning something new. Maybe you've always wanted to take up printmaking to create reproducible versions of your illustrations, or you've been dying to attend a lecture by a master filmmaker. Whether learning something brand new or getting a refresher on a topic you haven't touched in years, adding more knowledge to your repertoire, whether or not it directly relates to your field, is sure to bring new and exciting ideas that hadn't previously occurred to you.

Working alone can affect even the best of us. While it's great to be in full control of your surroundings, there's also no one to bounce ideas off when you need it most. So take the opportunity to ask for feedback from other freelance friends and provide the same sounding board for them when they need it. Or take advantage of blogs, forums, and social networking sites where other creatives openly share and ask for advice and feedback. It may seem weird at first, but remember that there are so many others out there just like you who benefit from this reciprocal feedback and community atmosphere. And attend networking events that allow you to meet fellow freelancers in person; not only will it give you the opportunity to chat with others in the same boat but you may even make a new friend or two.

When you start to view your office as a place of constant demands, it's easy to focus on the negatives—the bills that are due, the clients you can't stand, or the overwhelming number of items on your to-do list. Give yourself a break, both mentally and physically. Take a few days off, spend time at your favorite bookstore, or take the afternoon off. Finally, don't be so hard on yourself when things aren't going exactly as you'd like. When you're feeling burned out, consider all the great things you've accomplished and how far you've come. Remember that creative blocks are temporary.

ARE YOU A WORKAHOLIC?

If you subscribe to the notion that "time is money," you might be running yourself ragged by working all hours to ensure a lifeline stays hooked up to your bank account. But what about the lifeline to your social or family life, not to mention your leisure or downtime? Keeping pace in this lane of the rat race can be exhausting when your hours are under your own control and demand for your work increases. You may love the fact that no one is watching over you while you toil away, but there's also no one shutting off the lights and telling you to call it a day. Working hard is absolutely beneficial for your business, but it's detrimental when your personal life suffers as a result. Here are some telltale signs that you just might be a workaholic:

01 Your family eats dinner without you multiple times a week because of the late hours you're keeping.

02 Your friends don't invite you to social gatherings anymore, because they're tired of being turned down in favor of your looming deadlines.

03 You check e-mail from your cell phone while out to dinner, watching TV, or lying in bed.

04 You can't fall asleep at night, or you wake up in the middle of the night thinking about a project or client.

05 You find yourself talking about work all the time.

06 You often miss birthdays, anniversaries, and other important dates and events.

If one or more of these qualities applies to you, you may be burning the candle at both ends. Understandably, freelancing is more than just a career. It's a lifestyle that surrounds you daily and can consume your thoughts. But it shouldn't give you license to immerse yourself completely in work.

ANDREW ALMETER, ALMETER DESIGN

Graphic Designer | Brooklyn, NY

After eight years at three different graphic design firms, autonomy seemed to be the logical next step left for Andrew Almeter. Since starting Almeter Design in 2006, Andrew has amassed an impressive list of clients, including IMG Fashion/Mercedes-Benz Fashion Week, the Smithsonian Institution, and the Strong Buzz, as well as a smattering of popular New York restaurants. Despite having a steady stream of projects, Andrew has mastered the work-life balance. Several times a week, Andrew makes it a point to take hour-long bike rides during lunch. And every year, he takes a vacation to destinations across the globe, including a month-long stay in Buenos Aires. He shows us that it is possible to have a strong client base without being a complete workaholic, and that it's okay to say no to projects. Indeed, for Andrew, freelancing is more than just a career, but a lifestyle.

Who was your first freelance client, and how did you land that job?

My first freelance client was Tao Restaurant. After my last employer closed, they referred me to Tao. I've been lucky that most (if not all) of my work has come from referrals. It really pays to maintain good relationships with past employers and coworkers. As soon as you tell former colleagues about your new venture, you'd be surprised how many will refer you for potential jobs.

What makes you decide to turn down a job?

Overall, I value my time and don't make huge concessions in price. It's not just about money, but also about the type of work. I'll take on a job I'm excited about for less money if it's a really cool project or if it will allow me to tap into a new industry.

When interacting with a potential new client, trust your gut. If I know I'm not going to enjoy the process, I will turn down the job. Also I want to work with people who have an appreciation for design to begin with and whom I don't have to convince why design will benefit their company. If there is a client I don't want to work with, I'll tell them I don't think the project is the right fit and try to refer someone who could work well with them.

In the end, it's all about good karma. If you turn down someone politely and responsibly, they may even end up referring you to another client who is amazing.

Do you have any time management tips for working solo?

Learn to accept and work with your personal schedule as much as you can. In my case, I'm not a morning person. I may not wake up until 10 A.M., but then I tend to work until 12 or 1 A.M. Rather than trying to force myself into being an early riser, I schedule important meetings after 11 A.M., when I'm at my best. I also love the physical aspect of crossing things off a list, so while I have my full schedule online, I also have a notebook of handwritten to-do's for the day, which I manually cross off as they get done.

With such a busy workload, how do you go about including long lunch breaks and even longer vacations?

When you work from home, your surroundings can get old very quickly. Traveling and time away inspires and refreshes me, so I have to force myself to take little breaks and mini escapes from work whenever possible. It's a form of stress relief as well. Time management is key to being able to justify time off. As long as you know that you can finish your projects in time, there's no reason you shouldn't give yourself a break. For me to take that time off, I need to have some security for when I get back—whether it's money saved in the bank or work that's already lined up for when I return. Luckily, I have regularly scheduled assignments that have allowed me to plan my work schedule for the whole year, so I know when I might have free time for a vacation. Also, a vacation doesn't have to be completely about leisure. My last trip to Paris was a working vacation, but I managed my time so that I could also enjoy the experience and what the city had to offer.

If you establish good relationships with your clients and they know they can rely on the quality of your work, they're more likely to feel confident that their project will be completed despite any vacation plans you may have. When you know that you can come back to it and finish what needs to be done in a timely manner, you'll feel less guilty for getting away. It's absolutely crucial to have these mind and body reprieves from the stress of working every day.

What suggestions can you give to aspiring graphic designers who don't have a degree in the field?

To be a good designer, the ability and sensitivity to observe the world around you is so important. You need to reflect on what's going on in the world and within your industry. If you don't have an art background, read about design and art history to soak up things from the past. An understanding of and appreciation for past periods, styles, and history is so important to reference when looking toward the future of design. Also, just because you can use various design programs does not make you a designer. I strongly believe that typography skills are crucial for being a good graphic designer. Take classes and read books on the subject to really learn the nuances of type. Having that knowledge is essential, since graphic design is all about taking type and image and creating something new within these existing elements.

What's next for Almeter Design?

My next step is to expand, literally, by getting a separate space from home. I currently hire additional help with a summer intern each year and freelancers as needed. So my next step is to bring in a full-time designer as things continue to grow. In terms of new work, I'd love to create a product or something fun for kids like a children's book. I would love to expand my client base and do work for a boutique hotel, new museum, or some sort of cultural institution, or find a way to mix design with my love of travel. In the end, it's about surrounding yourself with things you love and love to do.

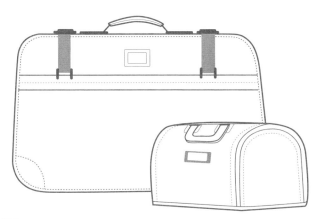

Me Time

We hear there was once an idyllic time in American life when you would sit under the comfortable shelter on your porch and unwind after a hard day's work with a tall glass of lemonade. Nowadays it seems that we eschew that sort of downtime and remain permanently connected to our cell phone and computer, not giving ourselves enough time to connect with ourselves. Even though freelancing can sometimes be an exhausting, all-consuming ride, you have to remember that it offers the flexibility to fit in personal time whenever you want. For once, you decide when and how to make your personal life a priority. Take advantage of your flexible schedule to take those trips you've always dreamed about. Your flexibility affords you the option to take whatever length of vacation you want. As long you plan ahead and know that your clients' needs are being met while you're away, take that two-week trip to Paris, a long weekend at the beach, or simply relish the quiet enjoyment of doing absolutely nothing for a day.

When project demands linger in your mind, you sometimes can't help but take them into your personal life. Before you call it a day, or a few times a week, find a mental escape that immerses you in an activity that takes your mind off things. Whether it's attending a rock climbing clinic or enrolling in a cooking class, find something that excites you and makes you look forward to that break. With all the stress you'll be putting on your body by sitting in front of a computer or standing behind a camera for hours on end, your body needs rest and reprieve from the daily grind—so exercise is always a good option. As it fuels your body, it will fuel your creative energy. Whatever hobby you choose, find something totally different from your work—this is a chance to escape that space, not sink more deeply into it.

The average American is said to have about sixteen hours of free time a week. Freelancers, we gather, probably have fewer. So spend that time with the people you love most. Make sure to incorporate your family and friends into your downtime and plan your work around them. Whether that means ending your workday when your spouse gets home, planning vacations around your kid's breaks from school, or turning off your cell phone when you're out to dinner with your boyfriend, make sure those most important to you feel like they are indeed a priority. After all, the biggest benefit to being a freelancer is the ability to mold your business into an ideal work situation that benefits both your business and personal life.

CHAPTER

8

NEXT STEPS

All businesses eventually reach a fork in the road, where one path leads to expansion and the other to extinction. Just like in any other business, for a freelancer, standing still or choosing neither path is hardly an option. In your first year of business, you'll learn how to manage your time and finances, build your client base, and win jobs—but you'll also encounter events that may shake your confidence. As you grow, you'll discover that the business you have now is not the business you had at the start. And that's not always a bad thing. In this chapter, you'll learn some cues that will help you determine when it's time to expand, collaborate, or, in some cases, call it quits. In the end, you'll find that success means different things to different people. Neither the size of your operation nor your bank account dictates success—only you can define what that means.

Your First Year

The first year of freelancing is a roller coaster of ups (scoring a big client), downs (getting rejected by your top-choice agent), and twists and turns (jobs taking you on unexpected paths). You probably underestimated a lot of things: the time and energy needed to start your freelance career, the burden of hidden business costs, the amount to charge your clients, or maybe, if you're fortunate, the overwhelming demand for your talent. And along the way, you probably encountered some surprises—discovering that you enjoy marketing your work or working without the constant presence of colleagues. On the flip side, maybe you discovered you actually don't like doing some of the things that you thought you would, such as working with a variety of clients or setting your own schedule. Starting a full-time freelance career will indeed come with a potpourri of lessons, learning experiences, and mistakes. They're all a natural part of the process. The important thing is to make adjustments based on the lessons you learned so you—and your business—can continue to thrive.

Should You Call It Quits?

In the first few years, it's natural to go through periods of doubt, burnout, or creative blockage. But these dark clouds should be temporary. If fighting these feelings becomes a daily battle, then that may be a sign that you need to reevaluate your freelance career. Here are some questions to ask yourself:

- Are you making enough money? While your business may not start out highly profitable, after a few years you should be earning a comfortable living and not living check to check. After several years, you should have earned enough to give yourself a vacation and save money for retirement.
- Are you motivated to work? Your work should energize you, but if you find yourself feeling bored, starting your workday later and later, and doing less work throughout the day for long stretches of time, you may be experiencing something more than simple burnout.
- Do you love producing your art for clients? Or do you find yourself limited by their needs and expectations?
- Has your quality of life improved? Freelancing affords you the ability to balance your work and personal life however you want. But if you've been unable to strike a balance, you may be allowing your work to take precedence over all other aspects of your life.

If you answered no to the majority of those questions, then it's time for some soul searching. Go back and figure out why you initially wanted to be a freelancer, and ask yourself if those reasons still apply. If you wanted to be a freelancer so that you could spend more time with your family, are you achieving that? If you went into freelancing for the independence, fame, or free time you thought it would bring you, do those reasons still seem compelling? When you start any business, including freelancing, failure is always a distinct possibility. Freelancing isn't for everyone. It may not live up to your expectations, or you might even miss the stability and the social interaction with coworkers that a nine-to-five gig often provides.

The key question at this point is, should you retreat or rebuild? If you decide you want to stick it out with freelancing, you should focus on what's next. While you can't control what brought you to this low point in your career, you can certainly control what comes next and steer your path in that direction. The best thing about starting over is, with adversity and hindsight come new perspectives and new ideas. Devote your comeback to focusing on the details of what you want to do differently this time around. Perhaps you don't want to design furniture but rather textile patterns. With your new plan, map out every obstacle you might encounter and devise ways to overcome them, so you won't find yourself in this rut again. Above all, don't keep negative feelings bottled up inside—or you'll start to believe the worst and will actualize the fears you have about yourself. You can control who gives you advice, so speak to people who are positive and will boost your confidence (yes, even your mom). It's important not to endure low points alone.

If you do consider returning to a full-time job, remember that it's not a fall from grace. There is no shame in wanting a steady paycheck to cover your rent or put food on the table. And even though the curtain has come down on your freelance career, remember that your talent is still alive and well. You can continue to practice your art on your own terms as a hobby or get a creative full-time job capitalizing on your newly honed skills. But before you hit the want ads, be sure to craft your résumé so that it directly applies to the new job you are applying for. Highlight skills you've acquired (such as your new Photoshop capabilities) or any achievements (such as an award in the I.D. Annual Design Review). In job interviews, talk about the growth and skills you've gained from working for yourself and how you've come full circle. You'll need to stress to potential new employers that you're returning to the on-staff workforce because you prefer working in a group setting or you enjoy the structure that a full-time job offers—not because you can't make ends meet. Employers are usually impressed with people who have gone solo and learned something new in the process. They'll respect your experience, but they also want to be sure you are coming back for the right reasons.

Once you do return to full-time status, be sure to let your clients know about the change. You can choose to offer your freelance services on the side, but inform them about your decreased availability. Or offer them a referral to a trusted freelancing colleague who would be a good replacement for you.

Should You Choose Growth?

It's practically impossible to handle a thriving business without changing or evolving. Over time, trends, market conditions, demand, technology, and, most important, you will change—and all those factors will affect your business. But what does growth mean? It could mean that you're increasing the size of your operation, offering additional services, expanding your client base, or going after bigger clients. Growth doesn't have to be in physical size; it can include growth in reputation and your ability to be more selective about the projects you do. You can grow in volume while staying the same size.

The best type of growth usually happens in a controlled, strategic manner and at a slow and steady pace. Grow too quickly and you'll likely find yourself in over your head, unable to meet your clients' needs, and possibly in debt. Then, what initially appears to be a lucky break can become an ordeal. If you don't adequately prepare for the increased demand and manage it as it grows, you can easily become overwhelmed and unable to capitalize on your own success. How big you want to grow is up to you. *Big* is a relative term. Do you want to be a creative director at the head of your own ten-person design studio? Or would you like to maintain a solo freelance career with the help of an assistant? As oxymoronic as it may seem, you can still grow and stay small. You can certainly keep your studio going by catering only to small and medium-size businesses or by taking on fewer projects with deeper budgets.

How do you plan for growth? Your first step would be to look at your present offerings and make a list of other services you'd like to explore. Some of the easiest services to expand into are those that are closely related to those you currently offer. Let's say you're a floral stylist who wants to offer additional services or capabilities. Ask yourself which new services are viable options and which you have interest in. For example, you might want to add food styling to your repertoire. But if you can't tell your cilantro from your parsley, you'll have to brush up on your foodie knowledge. Research which areas hold the most promise in your market and would likely provide the most rewards both artistically and financially.

. . . remember that as a freelancer it's not necessarily about building wealth, but about the process of how wealth is built.

Of course, you won't always be able to make plans for growth in advance. When success comes swiftly, you need to avoid being swept away by the tide. To quickly react to the demands of your market, you may be forced to craft plans just as quickly. If you find yourself in such a situation, remember that as a freelancer it's not necessarily about building wealth, but about the process of how wealth is built. For creatives, wealth does not always equal happiness, so be sure you are still being creatively fulfilled as you grow. For example, if you are approached by a mass merchandising company that wants to license your designs for children's backpacks, notebooks, and folios, you need to decide if accepting that offer would be consistent with your brand. Would it give your brand more reach or reduce it to homogeneity through overexposure? Consider these questions carefully, because if you say yes too quickly, you may find yourself and your business moving in a direction you don't like. When you become reactive instead of proactive about your career, it could push your career down a path that you never expected or wanted. So growing also means learning to sometimes say no. Ultimately, your business is an expression of you. So, grow your business, but stay true to yourself.

TEACHING

Freelancers are masters of juggling multiple projects. After you've spent some time in your solo career, you may be looking for an additional creative outlet or simply an additional source of income. Teaching your craft to others can be a great next step for those who enjoy the social and collaborative aspects of interacting with other creatives, and it can be done in unison with your freelance career.

If you're interested in teaching, you may want to try a practice run by hosting animation or photography workshops at your studio or by hiring a student intern for a semester. You'll get a sense of whether you have the patience and people skills to teach others, as well as what age group you might find most interesting to work with. Teaching young children can offer you the chance to pare down your methods to the basics and give your students ways to explore the world creatively without worrying about real-world applications. Think pinhole cameras and basic explorations of shape and color. If college students seem like a better fit, you'll be able to offer these students a more detailed and pragmatic approach to your art.

Teaching can offer you a new way to approach your own creativity. Whether you're a guide for five-year-olds or twenty-five-year-olds, you'll be surprised by how much you gain from their excitement about and innocence of the world and even their art. At the same time, your knowledge will offer them a perspective that not only enriches their learning experience but also gives them a taste of what they can expect in their future professional lives.

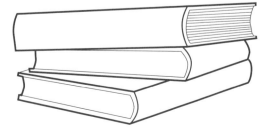

Sometimes your freelance career is handed to you on a platter when you least expect it. As unlikely as that may sound, it happened to Josh Owen. After graduating from the Rhode Island School of Design with an MFA in furniture design, Josh initially sought full-time positions as an industrial designer. But in interview after interview, companies instead offered him freelance opportunities to help with other designers' projects. When the search for a full-time position proved fruitless, he started to accept those freelance offers to generate some cash flow and, he hoped, land a full-time position with one of his clients. He found himself with a mixed bag of projects, from designing furniture to designing interiors, and eventually what began as a means to an end grew into a business. Over the past ten years, Josh has scored clients such as Areaware, Casamania, Kikkerland, and Umbra. And his list of accolades is equally impressive: Josh was the youngest designer in the Denver Art Museum's critically acclaimed show *American Design, 1975–2000*, and *Surface* magazine named him one of the most avant-garde industrial designers in the United States. Having grown up with a professor for a father, it wasn't long before Josh caught the teaching bug. He's now a professor at Philadelphia University, inspiring the next generation of industrial designers.

Would you recommend freelancing immediately out of school, or do you feel it's important to first work for a design studio?

Despite my own experience, I strongly suggest working for others in a full-time capacity first. Working full time allows you to learn from others' mistakes instead of your own—I wish I had had that opportunity. However, I do believe it is possible for young designers to find freelance success right out of school. It takes careful planning, tireless engagement, attention to detail, and an iron stomach.

As a freelance industrial designer, do you recommend selling your designs on your own or partnering with a larger company?

I've certainly seen individuals develop, self-produce, market, and distribute their own designs. It can be the most lucrative way to go. However, it can also be the most labor intensive and time consuming, not to mention the most challenging, because of all of the responsibility involved. In addition, in order to lessen the financial burden, some take on partners for capital. But this quickly blurs the boundaries between the individual and a corporate approach. The alternative, and my preference, is to receive royalties from a design that you worked on together with an established company, which is different from your typical work-for-hire freelance project.

How has your freelance business expanded or changed since you first started?

I now do more than just product design for my collaborative companies; I help them discover opportunities to develop their brand presence. I will often help them with their graphic presence, both print and virtual, and with strategic planning. The former helps to focus the meaning of a product within the context of the company, as well as its external positioning. The latter can encompass what venues to present the work in, whom to partner with, and how to discuss the project with the media. This kind of activity can become a mix of royalty and retainer.

You have some notable clients. Did they approach you, or did you approach them? What suggestions do you have for designers anxious to get their work picked up by larger companies?

It was combination of both. I have approached companies, and they have approached me. Sometimes sending samples and proposals can work, but I always hope to find a personal connection to start the conversation. Emerging designers should use their networks to do this. Professors, project sponsors, or internship mentors who know you well will often make introductions if they can.

As for how to get your work picked up, publish or perish by doing competitions and exhibiting your work. I often look for competitions on Core77.com and designboom.com, as both list most national as well as international opportunities. Also for emerging designers, *I.D.* magazine has a "concept" category, which can be a great venue. They are commonly respected venues that offer real challenges and test your ability to deliver meaningful ideas. This makes them good exercises regardless of the outcome and, often, they are juried by respected individuals in the field.

Winning is not everything. Regardless of the outcome, competitions increase the likelihood that a company will approach you or be interested when you approach them as you gain more credibility in your industry. One of those jurors may become a champion of your work, and that could pay back in dividends later.

Finally, exhibit your work whenever possible. These days, online venues are a click away. Core77.com hosts an outstanding portfolio section—all of my students post work there. There are opportunities to create pop-up exhibitions during the major industry fairs, such as ICFF [International Contemporary Furniture Fair] in New York City, SaloneSatellite at the Salone del Mobile in Milan, and Designphiladelphia in Philly. All are excellent venues for young designers. Exhibiting increases your exposure and likelihood of press. And these days, the media can very quickly rocket well-received work in the public sector into all sorts of spheres of influence.

How has teaching influenced your own work? What are the benefits of teaching while having your own business?

For me, being an educator is an act of social responsibility. Each day at the university I bring my experiences as a professional to bear with my students. It shapes their perceptions about the real world and makes them better prepared for it. I enjoy working with students; they bring fresh, contemporary eyes to the world, and I sleep better at night knowing that I give them my all so that they can navigate the complexities that they will encounter. And they challenge me! So I stay sharp. It is immensely gratifying.

As a teacher who designs, I feel my greatest potential contribution may come from mentoring students. In a world filled with too much already, our students must become filters and curators—this is almost as important as being form-givers or conduits connecting culture and commerce. As a designer who teaches, I'm afforded the opportunity to have more leeway to choose my professional projects carefully and pursue what I hope moves the global dialogue forward, as opposed to being pressured to create in order to put food on my family's table.

Partnering

There's only so much you can do yourself. In time, you may consider partnering or collaborating with another creative, outsourcing creative work, or even hiring staff to help lighten your workload. Partnering is, essentially, two or more people combining their efforts and assets to form a company. As for legal structure, you can choose a partnership, LLC (limited liability corporation), or a corporation, all of which are explained at the Small Business Administration's Web site (see Resources). Also, ask your accountant what's the best option for you. The good thing about getting a partner is that you'll be combining your clientele, reputation, and talents while providing moral and creative support for each other. A partner can also afford you the option to take vacations, since she can be trusted to manage the operation while you're away. Working with others can reduce feelings of loneliness, which are common among independent workers. And when you're working with a good person who is talented and affable, it can bring a new energy to your workplace. But is it worth losing your independence? When you have a partner, you have to share in the decision-making. Many times it can be helpful to bounce ideas off another person and feel strengthened by a decision when two people are behind it. However, with regard to the vision and direction of the company, you'll have to continually compromise and negotiate with your partner to make sure both visions are being satisfied.

You can form a partnership, in the legal sense of the term, without any formal agreement. But it's best to get it on paper, signed by the partners, dictating how responsibilities will be divided, which assets and contributions each partner is providing, how you will share in the profits, and what your goals are. Even if you're best friends—and perhaps especially if you're best friends—always have an outline of grievance procedures should the partnership dissolve.

Working successfully with a partner is all about balance. Divide and conquer by defining each person's roles in the company based on his or her talents, strengths, and weaknesses. Some roles may seem more obvious than others. For example, if you're a motion graphics designer and your counterpart is a photographer, the roles are evident in the creative process. However, if one person is better known for marketing prowess and the other for organizational acumen, then the first partner should be in charge of interacting with clients and landing new jobs for the business, while the second should be responsible for organizing finances and scheduling. As with anything, it may take some trial and error to strike the best balance, so try on different hats until you both find the best fit for each of you.

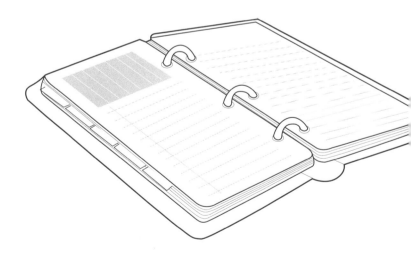

POWER COUPLE

Charles and Ray Eames. Kate and Andy Spade. Mark Badgley and James Mischka. Couples engaged as a successful creative-business team can be a powerful—and rare—collaboration. They come with the distinct advantage of having shared experiences (good and bad), but sharing a bed doesn't always make sharing a company easy. As in any partnership, discuss your individual and joint goals before diving in headfirst. It's critical to be on the same page from the get-go. And as we mentioned in the Partnering section, you should clearly define each of your roles. You both may have the talent to photograph beautiful images, but maybe you're the one who best handles the big clients, while your husband works on your brand and generates the marketing program. It's also important to talk about what might happen if the partnership—romantic or professional—doesn't work out. Clearly, there are both emotional and financial risks involved. What's Plan B if you decide you can't work together after all? It's far better to acknowledge and address these possibilities when you're starting out than to wait until you're immersed in the business.

As a working couple, you'll also face the challenges of maintaining professional decorum in the workplace during stressful times and preserving the sanctity of your personal life. You should treat your partner as you would a fellow employee, which means keeping the pillow talk out of the studio and knocking on your partner's office door before barging in. At the same time, you should try to keep the shop talk at work and not let it overflow into your personal life. Nurture your relationship with weekly dates or outings where it's just about relaxing and having fun. Also, when you're spending time with someone 24/7, it'll become more important to spend time apart as well.

One of the biggest advantages you'll have as a couple is complete trust in each other—you know, when making decisions, that your partner will always have your best interest and your company's best interest in mind. Husband-and-wife team Rebecca Thuss and Patrick Farrell of ThussFarrell (a design and photography studio) admit, "We have a healthy competition with one another, but it never takes a nasty turn. Friendly competition is good because it keeps you striving to be better at what you do. We still can never quite understand each other's process, but both are relevant and both approaches create a stronger result." A shared business can certainly strengthen your bond as you learn together, encounter successes and failures together, and make plans for world domination together.

When it comes to finding a compatible business partner, sometimes you needn't look further than your bedroom. This was certainly the case for Amanda Woodward and her husband/business partner, Dana Woodward. Though Amanda had taken the freelancing leap first, launching Woodward Design in 2003, within a couple years she found herself with a growing workload she could no longer handle on her own. For her, it made sense to find a partner to help support the company's growth. The search was easy enough, as her husband, Dana, was also a practicing graphic designer. For the Woodwards, partnering and collaborating creatively was actually a manifestation of a dream they'd had since their days at Grant MacEwan College. What they discovered as a team was that their strong personal relationship resonated in their business practices. For Amanda and Dana, growth is about putting a premium on what's important to you, and in their case, it's about staying local and building relationships with clients.

Who was your first freelance client, and how did you land that job?

Amanda: My first freelance client was a local theater company called Northern Light Theatre. The story isn't too romantic. They basically put an ad in a local arts newspaper looking for a designer, so I responded and got the job. The best part about it is, we still work for them. In fact, this is our ninth season with the theater group. We don't just do design work for them; we also donate a lot of our time to their organization. We enjoy being involved in what they're doing. We've built such a good relationship with them that I can call the art director a friend at this point.

It sounds like most of your clients are local. Do you find that your proximity is something your clients appreciate?

Dana: Most of our clients are local clients, though we occasionally have some clients from eastern Canada and the U.S. as well. For us, one thing we enjoy about our job is developing relationships with our clients. We find that our clients tend to respond to us really well in person, so being able to meet face to face is a plus.

When did Dana become a partner in Woodward Design?

Amanda: We've always had desires and dreams to collaborate. After starting Woodward Design, I wanted him to eventually join me, but we knew it would definitely be a risk for two of us to go solo. It was scary enough with one of us not having a steady income. Plus, Dana worked at a boutique design studio and loved his job. He knew he would miss working with all of his buddies there.

Dana: The turning point was when Amanda was being considered for a large contract in 2005. She knew she wouldn't be able to do it by herself. So we made a deal: if she gets this gig, then I would quit. As you can probably tell, we got the contract, and the rest just fell into place.

How do you define each of your roles in the company?

Amanda: In general, we split the workload fairly evenly—there is a lot of overlap in terms of tasks we do. And we both have our own clients that we manage. But we do have certain roles that capitalize on our strengths. For instance, I take care of proposal writing, invoicing, and money-related tasks. I'm also trained as an illustrator, so naturally I do the illustration work. Dana is strong in developing logos and identities. He also tends to manage clients that need more hand holding or more meetings and phone conversations, since he has a great personality. He's very patient and works well with those types of clients.

What are some of the advantages to being a couple that works together? What are some of the challenges?

Amanda: When working with Dana, a certain comfort level already exists. It's much different than conversing with a colleague, where there are boundaries and you need to act professional all the time. We have a pretty up-front way of working with each other—we're very candid when we critique each other's work. This honesty has allowed me to grow as a designer.

Dana: With regard to the relationships we have with our clients, I think that being a couple in business tends to make people feel more comfortable with us as a business. It just evokes a more personal feeling. But a disadvantage to working together is that it can be tricky to turn off work at the end of the day. It can be unhealthy to let shop talk consume so many hours in our day. When we go on vacation, we have to remember to not talk about work and remind each other to just relax!

We see you also have an employee as well. What was the reason behind hiring someone?

Amanda: We hired a graphic designer about two years ago. It was largely a workload issue—we definitely needed some extra help! At the time, we were planning to take a six-week road trip across Canada. In order to take that vacation, we needed someone to run the day-to-day of the business and be able to hold down the fort. We were looking for someone with experience in graphic design, a good design aesthetic, and ultimately someone we were comfortable with and could trust, since this person would be coming to our house and getting a key to our front door.

How do you find interesting work, or does it find you usually? Do you do any promotional activity for your work?

Dana: We've gotten most of our work through word of mouth and referrals. Our reputation for the most part keeps jobs coming. Our Web site has also been a really good marketing tool for generating inquiries. But one day we do hope that we can spend some time pinpointing businesses we want to work with and contacting them—we just haven't gotten to that point yet. Amanda: We do promotional activities to appreciate our current clients, because those are the clients that keep referring us. For example, on our fifth anniversary, we had a party at a wine bar for our clients where we raffled off some of my illustrations. Last holiday season, I baked homemade granola and placed it in wooden boxes and sent them to fifty of our best clients. I think when you put in that extra touch to nurture your existing relationships, clients appreciate it.

If you could start your business over, is there anything you would do differently?

Amanda: I wish I had been open to hiring someone sooner. I remember all those nights where I stayed up until 2 A.M. Looking back, it seems silly that I put myself through that. When you are doing everything, it's hard to let go of control. I was trying to do it all on my own, and it was so stressful, but it all worked out in the end. When you finally make the decision to hire someone, you'll wonder why you didn't do it sooner.

Collaborating and Outsourcing

To join forces with a creative without relinquishing your business independence, try collaborating on a project-by-project basis. For some freelancers, such as film producers or graphic designers, your role is akin to a general contractor hiring the right people to do the work—so collaborating and outsourcing will be pretty commonplace. Indeed, collaborating with other freelancers in other fields is a great way to offer your clients additional services that complement yours. For example, if you're a print graphic designer and your client wants a Web site to match the identity you've created for the company, but you don't know a lick of HTML to save your life, that presents the perfect opportunity to collaborate with a Web designer. You'll have to find someone you can trust to create a Web site that looks professional and cohesive with your print materials. Once you find the right person to collaborate with, he just may become your point person for future Web design needs—and vice versa, as he can return the favor when one of his clients needs print materials.

If you need someone to fill in during a temporary crunch, it might make more sense to farm the work out to another freelancer than to hire someone permanently.

What if you just have more projects than you can handle? If you need someone to fill in during a temporary crunch, it might make more sense to farm the work out to another freelancer than to hire someone permanently. You'll need to find someone who is suitable for the project and available to complete it in the time allowed. Trust your instincts and be wary of any red flags, because their work will ultimately reflect on your reputation. You'll need to create a project brief, a set of deadlines, and a schedule for how payments will be made, and you'll need to draft a contract for the work. Much like the contract described in chapter 5, this agreement should state the deliverables, due dates, payments, and terms that both you and the subcontracted party have agreed upon. Your client does not need to know that you've brought in other freelancers to help you with the workload as long as they are only assisting the project, and you are still acting as head creative.

Hiring Staff

Do you find yourself spending too much time on routine tasks or perhaps neglecting your paperwork and bookkeeping? Do you need an assistant stylist or photographer to fill the creative demands of your clients? Depending on your answer, you may need to hire an administrative aide or bring on another creative. But the decision to hire staff is not one to take lightly. You have to decide whether you can afford the payroll for an employee, whether there is enough of a workload, and even whether there is enough space in your studio. You'll also need to provide your employee with the tools, furniture, and equipment necessary for a comfortable and efficient work environment. Instead of merely planning your day and your week, you'll have to make sure you have work lined up for your new employee until she is able to manage herself. And, since you've probably gotten used to being alone, you might find it hard to delegate tasks to others.

Then again, even though salaries can take a big bite out of your pocket and, initially, your time, having staff can increase your productivity and efficiency, giving you a greater capacity to take on new work. It can allow you to serve your clients better and, ultimately, improve your position in the industry.

Don't feel threatened—hiring someone with more skills or talent is a way to ensure growth in your business. She may have ideas that can take your company in directions you hadn't quite considered.

From an economic standpoint and when hiring for the first time, it's best to hire someone at an entry-level position, rather than trying to properly pay a candidate who has had a previous salaried experience. Start a new employee on a part-time schedule if you are unsure of the amount of work to go around. You should hire someone whose skills and abilities you lack or someone to do tasks you no longer have time for. If you have to hire another creative talent, make sure that person is as talented as, if not better than, you. Don't feel threatened—hiring someone with more skills or talent is a way to ensure growth in your business. She may have ideas that can take your company in directions you hadn't quite considered. Consequently, you may be able to offer more services and high-quality work to your clients.

And don't feel that hiring someone who's talented will lead to quick turn-over in the job. As long as you provide an environment and workload that employee finds challenging, fun, and comfortable, she will be less likely to jump back out in search of a new gig.

Finally, a prospective employee can look great on paper but, ultimately, you need to like him as a person and foresee being able to get along with him. You'll likely be spending a lot of time with this person in a small space, so you'll want to enjoy this time and feel a mutual respect between the two of you.

Offering Internships

Hiring an intern offers you a short-term glimpse at what having a full-time employee would be like. You will get a new, youthful perspective and, hopefully, someone who makes you more productive. Interns can bring enthusiasm and energy to your workplace, and they can do things that you are often too busy to do. And because your home studio may be one of their first working experiences, interns may be more open to less-than-traditional working environments. However, they also need more hand-holding and direction than someone with real-world experience, so be sure you have the time and patience. Focus on recent graduates or student interns who are nearing completion of their degrees (i.e., juniors or seniors), because they are more likely to have stronger skill sets than those just starting their art-school education. You can post your internship requirements on job boards at local schools. Make sure to spell out the qualities and skills the potential intern must possess, so that you target those who are most likely to suit your needs.

Interns can be paid or unpaid, but if you choose to go the unpaid route, it's wise to offer your internship for school credit. Credit requirements differ for each school's internship programs (most usually require a minimum amount of internship hours per week) but you should try to fulfill all the requirements so your interns can earn credit while you reap the rewards of their enthusiasm and assistance. If you choose to accept postgraduate interns, that can be an opportunity to "audition" them before bringing them on as entry-level hires.

You'll likely receive a good number of applicants for your intern position, so pick those with the most promise and schedule an in-person interview. Usually after an in-person meeting you'll have a good sense of the candidate's work, talent, and personality. Also, take note of whether he was late or dressed inappropriately for your meeting. Tardiness can give you a clue into how he may behave when working, and inappropriate attire could signal a level of unprofessionalism that you might not want to bring in to your studio.

One way to avoid making a mistake is to set a two-week trial period, during which you can evaluate the candidate's performance.

Because you can't really anticipate how a candidate will actually perform once hired—even after a successful interview—choosing one can be a bit of a guessing game. One way to avoid making a mistake is to set a two-week trial period, during which you can evaluate the candidate's performance. It offers you the chance to cut your losses before getting in too deep, and it gives the candidate a chance to see if your internship is what he had hoped for. If a candidate proves to be a good fit with your business, set a schedule of how many days per week and hours per day you'd like him to work. You may need only part-time assistance at first and can gradually increase each successive intern's hours as your needs grow.

It should be noted, though, that interns should not be treated like indentured servants. If they've interned at your studio to learn the ropes of creating an animation storyboard, they shouldn't spend most of their days filling coffee requests. Depending on your needs and her schedule, an intern may work with you anywhere from ten to forty hours per week. By the end of an internship period (usually a semester long, or two to four months), your intern should have gained experience, insight into the industry, new skills, and something noteworthy to add to her résumé or portfolio while having assisted you in the daily tasks of running your business. Internships are best when the experience is beneficial to both parties.

How to Be a Good Employer and Boss

01 Set clear and distinct roles and responsibilities. While there can certainly be crossover on responsibilities, each individual should be responsible for his own tasks.

02 Rotate leadership roles among the members of your creative staff so they can try out different roles and play new parts in the team dynamic.

03 Find work that will energize your creative staff. Workers want to feel challenged and motivated. Listen to your employees to learn about what excites them—you'll be able to hear it in their voices if they're engaged with the work you're giving them.

04 Have your staff generate side projects that interest them, whether developing the company's blog or taking fun staff photos for the company Web site.

05 Provide constant communication and feedback. Employees want to know they are doing a good job, so tell them. Similarly, you need to develop ways of giving constructive criticism. Otherwise, employees will never be sure exactly where they stand with you.

06 Provide a comfortable working environment. Chances are if you enjoy coming to your work space, they will too.

07 Create trust and expect the same in return. If your employees are working in your home, trust is extra important—you'll want to feel comfortable giving them keys or access to your space.

08 Empower your creative staff to be themselves and give them freedom to follow their creative vision.

09 Show respect for their ideas. Allow employees the opportunity to contribute in meetings, brainstorming sessions, photo shoots, and critiques.

10 Give them credit for the work they created. Whether it's a byline on an article, an illustration credit, or letting your client know an employee had a hand in creating the final product, let your employees get public recognition for their work.

11 Work as a team. Show your employees that you'll do whatever they do, including taking out the garbage. No task is beneath you.

12 Don't overwork your employees. Allow them to have some downtime to recharge by encouraging daily lunch breaks and regular vacations.

Long-Term Success Strategies

Your business should focus on more than merely surviving—it should focus on thriving. Reflect on the positives of where you are now, how far you've come, and where you see yourself headed. Continue with the choices you've made that have worked in your favor and learn from your mistakes to push forward toward growth and increased success. Regardless of your own wins and losses, continue to stay relevant and treat your business with the same passion you had from day one.

Continue meeting people

Even if you've established a tight network of colleagues or a good list of clients, you should always continue to meet people and make connections. You never know where a new connection can lead, both personally and professionally.

Continue to build and promote your brand

Over time, your company will grow and evolve, and so should your brand. Examine even the smallest detail of your brand, covering all visual and verbal interactions. Reexamine everything from your Web site and your logo to how you answer your phone. Even your mission statement will likely change, and you should revisit and update it regularly.

Widen your customer base

If you decide to hire full-time staff because you landed a huge client, what would happen should that client cancel the job? Do not rely on a single client to provide paychecks for your entire company. Make sure you have a broad base of clientele to provide constant work for the staff you have.

Don't forget about customer retention

As you'll learn with time, landing a client is sometimes easier than keeping one. Because buyers often come to freelancers for a one-time project, it's common to work with them for months on end and then infrequently after that. Do your best to maintain relationships with your current and past clients. They'll be more likely to keep you in mind when a new project comes up and to refer you to other potential customers.

Stay ahead of the curve

Perhaps you're a music video director who's presented a new style or aesthetic to the market—and established a new trend. As with all trends, competitors will catch on, and soon other directors will be copying your style ad nauseam. There's usually not much you can do about it, so continue to evolve and stay ahead of the copycats. Plus, your clients and fans will want to see what new ideas you come up with.

Take a proactive stance in your career

If you've become popular for creating work in a particular aesthetic, you may find yourself with a steady stream of clients asking for the same thing. When a certain style of your work catches on, it's easy to be complacent and simply fill the demand. If you find this happening, ask yourself if the work you're producing is a direction in which you want continue. Maybe it's a style of illustration that is particularly tedious, and you've come to realize that it's too difficult to meet the demand. Remember that it's up to you to show clients clear examples of the type of work you want to do; otherwise, they will continue to want what they see. Grab your business by the reins and provide direction, lest it take on a life of its own.

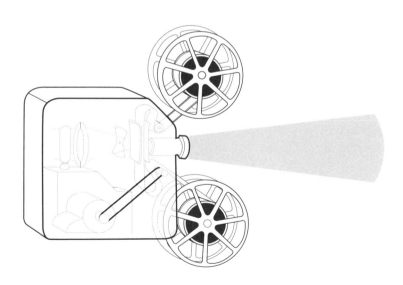

The Future Awaits

Just like the *Choose Your Own Adventure* books from pop culture past showed, there really are numerous paths your freelance career can take. Whether you travel through Door #1 or Door #2, you'll no doubt encounter some ups and downs. You may encounter problematic vendors or lose that competition in which you hoped to place—all the while landing your dream client and watching the demand for your work grow. But that's the beauty of it. Freelancing offers the unique opportunity to mold your job into whatever you want it to be. Work fifteen hours a week or fifty; have local clients or long-distance buyers; work from home or from a studio; stay solo or become a multiperson business. The choices are endless—and in your hands. And even if your career is sailing along, you have to remember that there is always room for improvement. Success, as you've read in the interviews in this book, is never bestowed; it is chased after, and those who are up to that challenge reap the rewards. And, though the rewards may be money and fame, those can be empty indeed if there is nothing personal at heart of your quest. So keep your eye on the prize, but don't forget the important things like family and friendships. In the end, our hope is that you'll have the building blocks for a successful freelance career, so that your work and quality of life become more fulfilling than ever.

Resources

Interviewees

Also, www.also-online.com
Amy Ruppel, www.amyruppel.com
Andrew Almeter, www.almeterdesign.com
Andrew Bannecker, www.andrewbannecker.com
Aviva Michaelov, www.nytimes.com
Chris Riehl, www.chris.weareborn.tv
Fox Tax Service, www.foxtaxservice.com
Josh Owen, www.joshowen.com
Lauren Shields, www.laurenshields.com
Lilla Rogers, www.lillarogers.com
Matt Armendariz, www.mattarmendariz.com
Nina Chakrabarti, www.ninachakrabarti.com
Sarah Laird, www.sarahlaird.com
Thayer Allyson Gowdy, www.thayerphoto.com
ThussFarrell, www.thussfarrell.com
Ward Jenkins, www.wardjenkins.com
Woodward Design, www.woodwarddesign.ca

Administrative Tools

Conference Genie (U.K.), www.conferencegenie.co.uk
eFax, www.efax.com
Free Conference, www.freeconference.com
Google Apps, www.google.com/apps
iChat, www.apple.com
Send6, www.send6.com
Skype, www.skype.com
Tictocit (invoicing & time tracking), www.tictocit.com
YouSendIt, www.yousendit.com

Freelancer Communities and Conferences

Creative Freelancer Conference, www.creativefreelancerconference.com
Directors Guild of America, www.dga.org
Freelancer's Union, www.freelancersunion.org

Freelance Switch, www.freelanceswitch.com
HOW Design Conference, www.howconference.com
ICON Illustration Conference, www.theillustrationconference.org
International Conference on Food Styling and Photography, www.bu.edu/
foodandwine/conference
PDN Photo Plus Expo, www.photoplusexpo.com
SXSW (film and interactive conference), www.sxsw.com

Competitions, Job Boards, and Portfolio Hosting Sites
Core77, www.core77.com
Coroflot, www.coroflot.com
Creative Hotlist, www.creativehotlist.com
Style Careers, www.stylecareers.com
Style Portfolios, www.styleportfolios.com
The Black Book, www.blackbook.com
Workbook, www.workbook.com

Financial Products and Services
FreshBooks, www.freshbooks.com
Mint, www.mint.com
PayPal, www.paypal.com
ProPay, www.epay.propay.com
QuickBooks, www.quickbooksgroup.com

Licensing and Trade Shows
George Little Management, www.glmshows.com
ICFF, www.icff.com
The International Textile Show, www.californiamarketcenter.com/latextile
PrintSource, www.printsourcenewyork.com
Surtex, www.surtex.com.com

Pricing Resources
AIGA | Aquent Survey of Design Salaries, www.designsalaries.org
The Graphic Artists Guild Handbook, www.graphicartistsguild.org

Professional Organizations

American Institute of Graphic Arts, www.aiga.org
The Art Directors Club, www.adcglobal.org
The Association of Illustrators, www.theaoi.com
ATypI, www.atypi.org
Creative Latitude, www.creativelatitude.com
Design Council, www.designcouncil.org.uk
Graphic Artists Guild, www.gag.org
Industrial Designers Society of America, www.idsa.org
The International Council of Graphic Design Associations, www.icograda.org
Professional Photographers of America, www.ppa.com
Society of Illustrators, www.societyillustrators.org
The Society of Publication Designers, www.spd.org

Protecting Your Work

Creative Commons, www.creativecommons.org
U.S. Copyright Office, www.copyright.gov
U.S. Patent and Trademark Office, www.uspto.gov

Small Business Assistance

Companies, Inc, www.companiesinc.com
Nolo, www.nolo.com
U.S. Small Business Administration, www.sba.gov

Small Business Forums and Communities

Biz Box, www.bizbox.slate.com
Biznik, www.biznik.com
Score, www.score.org
SmartBiz, www.smartbiz.com
Workaholics Anonymous, www.workaholics-anonymous.org

Social Portals and Blog Hosts

Blogger, www.blogger.com
Facebook, www.facebook.com
LinkedIn, www.linkedin.com
MySpace, www.myspace.com

TypePad, www.typepad.com
Twitter, www.twitter.com
Word Press, www.wordpress.com

Tax Information
U.S. Internal Revenue Service, www.irs.gov

Trade Publications and Annual Competitions
Communication Arts magazine, www.commarts.com
How magazine, www.howdesign.com
ID magazine, www.id-mag.com
PDN/Photo District News, www.pdnonline.com
Print magazine, www.printmag.com

Web Site Domains and Hosting
GoDaddy, www.godaddy.com
Network Solutions, www.networksolutions.com

Index

Acknowledgments

To our editors, Jodi Warshaw and Kate Woodrow, for championing this project, and for your advice throughout. To our agent, Lilly Ghahremani, for believing in our joint project and encouraging us to make it a reality. Special thanks to our assistants Virginia Dolen, Kimberly Kulka, and Andrea Rell for their dedicated research, proofreading, and taking care of everything around the studio so we could focus on writing. Thank you to Shane Abad at Disney and Andrew Beall at Pixar for insight into the film and animation industries. Our deepest gratitude is extended to Andrew Bannecker, Chris Riehl, Lauren Shields, Julia Rothman, Jenny Volvovski, Matt Lamothe, Thayer Allyson Gowdy, Matt Armendariz, Aviva Michaelov, Amy Ruppel, Mark Fox, Nina Chakrabarti, Lilla Rogers, Sarah Laird, Kenna Zimmer (on behalf of Sarah Laird), Ward Jenkins, Andrew Almeter, Josh Owen, Rebecca Thuss, Patrick Farrell, and Amanda and Dana Woodward. Thank you for taking the time to share your inspirational stories with us and giving us an inside look into your world and work.

Joy: To my husband, Bob, for being my best friend and unofficial (and unbashful) press rep and for always reminding me that everything works out in the end. To my brother, Jay, for being an awesome brother, period. To my brother-in-law, Vince, for your honest and valuable advice when I was just starting my freelance career. To my parents-in-law, Jackie and Sam, who may not know exactly what I do for a living but are always proud of me regardless. To my parents, Sunanta and Chumlong, for passing on your entrepreneurial spirit to me. You've encouraged me to be my own boss ever since I can remember, and taking your advice was one of the best things I've ever done. Finally, to my coauthor, Meg, you're the best partner in crime I could have asked for in writing in this book. Thanks for your never-ending humor and sarcasm, which always made our looming deadlines and crazy work days much more bearable.

Meg: To my husband, Marvin, who will probably find irony in chapter 7, thank you for your love and support especially at times when my career overwhelms our personal life. To my kids, Lauryn and Miles, for cracking me up all the time and being a constant source of inspiration. To my brother, Alden, who had nothing to do with this book and whom I see rarely, but who would get a great thrill out of seeing his name in print. To my parents, Alfonso and Dely, who still don't know how to explain what I do for a living to their friends but are proud of me anyway. Thanks especially for baby-sitting the kids so I could get work done. To Joy, for being the Shirley to my Laverne. Thank you for giving me a swift kick in the butt when deadlines were approaching and an even swifter kick when I missed them. I couldn't have asked for a better coauthor for this book.